THE LAURANZANO FAMILY

THE LAURANZANO FAMILY

From The Mountains Of Calabria

Enrico G Lauranzano

authorHOUSE®

AuthorHouse™
1663 Liberty Drive
Bloomington, IN 47403
www.authorhouse.com
Phone: 1-800-839-8640

First published by AuthorHouse   11/9/2009

ISBN: 978-1-4490-0189-6 (e)
ISBN: 978-1-4490-0188-9 (sc)

Library of Congress Control Number: 2009911093

Printed in the United States of America
Bloomington, Indiana

This book is printed on acid-free paper.

I dedicate this narrative to the memory of all our family members that passed on before us, in Italy as well as in America. They were all dearly beloved members of The Lauranzano Family and they will be remembered always.

In particular, I dedicate this to my sister Allie because she kept our family together when Pa and Ma were lost to us. She kept the family history and kept communications open with our kin in Italy. As one of the family members in Italy said when informed of Allie`s passing, "Allie was the soul of our family".

I love you, Allie, and I hope this book will reach you in heaven, where you are resting, and that you will be pleased with my effort, *well, maybe you won`t be all together pleased but at least I might deserve a "nice try, Rick".*

CONTENTS

Book II: Growing Up

Book III: Moving On

PREFACE

My name is Enrico George Lauranzano. I got the Enrico part of my name when I entered the Washington Elementary School in Beverly, Massachusetts in the year 1929 when my sister Allie brought me to school for the first time and told them that was my name. Since my birth name is Americo, I will tell you later why she did this. The George part I thought would be a cool name when I chose it at confirmation when someone told me that St George slew a dragon. The Lauranzano part was from my father, a brave and gallant man who led a life of sorrow, happiness, misery and adventure, and who originated the Lauranzano clan in this country.

I am going to write of my father's life in Italy as well as here in America and of his marriages and his offsprings, his sorrows and his joys. He struggled to make a life for us and I will write of his failures and his successes.

Now I'm not a writer by any stretch and I'm certain others could write of my father's life a lot better than I, but, when writing of my father's life you must also have the *desire* and the *love* for this man. I have an abundance of both of these qualifications, giving me two out of three of the qualifications.

The person who should be writing of my father's life is my late sister, Allie. She truly stayed with my father and mother her whole life and with certainty had a deep love for both and an abundance of memories to recall. Sad to say, Allie is no longer with us so I am going to try very hard to put my father's life and the Lauranzano family life in writing and in so doing, make Allie proud.

I want to assure anyone that reads this narrative that I have done a thorough research, here in America as well as in Italy and everything that I write here, to the best of my knowledge, is factual. All the photos are from Allie's collection, so without Allie's caring attitude for the past and her love for the family, these photos and much of our past would have been lost to us. She is not writing this, but she certainly is a part of the doing.

I write this because the future should know what happened to make their lives what it is. No matter where any of us go or do, it has to be influenced by the past. My father and mother came to America with nothing but hope and anxieties. They built a life for all of us here, in America, under very trying conditions and I will attempt to tell of this.

I hope you will enjoy reading it. Thank you.

INTRODUCTION

In Italia, at the turn of the twentieth century, the economy was at a dismal low. Very few Italians could find a job anywhere in Italia, particularly in the Region of Calabria and on the Island of Sicily, where citizens were literally starving. Italians were moving out of their areas and traveling anywhere in the country, seeking employment. This led to the overcrowding of unemployed citizens in the industrial areas of Italia, and they were becoming restless.

In order to relieve this condition, the government enacted a law that stated that a citizen was required to reside at least six months in a region before they were allowed to apply for any job, no matter how small or how important the job. One can only imagine how effective this law was or how helpful it was. Everyone that relocated had to return from whence they came and literally continue on the road to starvation. To begin with, how could a person without funds or means of support live in an area for six months, waiting to apply for a job that in all probability did not exist. Since an Italian was not allowed to petition for employment anywhere in Italia except within his native region, where there were no jobs, he would have to seek employment elsewhere.

As the potato famine in Ireland started Ireland's mass exodus in the 1860s, Italia's mass exodus started at the turn of the century, to seek employment. The Italian migration to America, where "the streets were lined with gold," was not to seek riches, as some would have you believe, but was only in an effort to find a paying job that would support a man's family. This is the story of such a man. His name is Natale Lauranzano, and his story must be told.

During this time of Natale's life, there were two preferred countries to which people immigrated. The most popular was The United States of North America, and second in popularity was Argentina of South America. The United States was the most popular with many Europeans, but the Southern Italians were leaving in big numbers for Argentina. My father chose to immigrate to the United States for no apparent reason other than, as he said, "the fare was cheaper."

Since my man had to work, scrimp, and save for years to accumulate lira enough to make the trip to America, any reduction that he achieved in the basic cost of the voyage could result in the equivalent of many years of saving and scrimping, so the United States it had to be. Much to his chagrin, he had to do it solo, leaving his life mate Maria behind, as many other men had to do in those early years. This was a heartbreaking experience for Natale. As he said many times, "It had to be done. It broke my heart, but I had to do it."

Natale and Maria were young, with many years ahead of them, so what did they have to lose but a little time together. She would live with her parents and "hold the fort" until he sent for her, and then they would "live like humans, in the land of opportunity." So, off he went. To save further lira, he walked the entire distance to the Port of Napoli. It was a very long walk, but he allowed himself enough time to get there and board with the remainder of the passengers, and to venture, literally, for parts unknown—but also for a future that he hoped and prayed would bring for him and Maria a life of prosperity and happiness.

Natale left Italy from the mountainous region of Calabria and the Comune di Verzino, which is located deep in the southern part of Italy on the Sili Greca Mountain Range. He had been twenty-one years of age when he married Maria Leo, also of Verzino, his childhood sweetheart. They married in the Comune di Verzino in the Chiesa Madre, the Comune's only church, on July 13, 1899. Four years later, in the year 1903, Natale departed Verzino to seek his fortune in the United States of America, the land that he hoped would offer him opportunity to support a family. He left Maria behind with the all-too-familiar promise heard throughout Europe in those days, "When I am settled in America and have enough money, I will send for you." He kissed his beloved Maria goodbye, walked down the mountain, and continued his walk all the way to the Port of Napoli, where he sailed on the Pheonicia with 1,700 other Calabrians.

It took almost a month at sea before Natale viewed the skyline of New York and arrived at Ellis Island. He did not know anyone on the ship and he did not meet anyone that he could call friendly. The trip was tiresome and lonely. He said that, many times during the journey, he cried because he missed Maria. In his later years, Natale did not like discussing that crossing. It brought back many bad memories that he would have liked to forget about.

Arriving at Ellis Island on May 2, 1903, there were throngs of people all around him, shouting out to relatives and friends in all possible languages. But he was all alone in a new country—where no one was expecting him, with nowhere to turn—and he was overwhelmed.

God bless you Pa, it's a brave, brave thing that you do.

THE LAURANZANO FAMILY

Book I: The Early Years

My father was born in the Comune di Verzino, which is located on the La Sili Greca Mountain Range, where he attended a church school through the eighth grade. After graduation from the eighth grade, he began working "down mountain" for despicable land owners, whom the peons (workers) called padrones. The padrones were notorious for treating the peons no better then they treated their animals. Verzino, around 1891, had a population of roughly 400 souls, with no clear or level land on which to earn a living. If you wanted the status quo and to not starve to death, you had no other choice but to go down mountain and apprentice to a hated padrone. Unfortunately, the young boys of Verzino were forced into this type of labor at the early age of ten to twelve, depending on the amount of schooling they had.

Natale was born to Giuseppe Giovanni Laurenzano (how he spelled the name) and Teresa De Luca. Their offspring, including Natale, were: Giuseppe Michele, the oldest, born September 28, 1873, in Longobucco; Caterina, born October 20, 1876, also in Longobucco; Natale, born January 26, 1878, in Verzino; and Salvatore Pasquale, born February 22, 1882, also in Verzino.

The senior Giuseppe Giovanni was born in Longobucco in 1847. He departed for Verzino from Longobucco, the city of his birth, with his spouse, Teresa (De Luca), and his two children, Giuseppe Michele, age four; and Caterina, age one. At the time, which was around 1877, Verzino had a population of approximately 50 souls, with no visible means of self-support.

Giuseppe Giovanni, the senior, could see right away that the recently arrived Laurenzano family had one very serious problem!

Verzino is located on the slope of a mountain, about a mile above sea level, and is isolated, two to three hours from humanity, even when traveling by express donkey. Verzino had once been a fiefdom, owned by one Nicola Cortese as recently as 1860. For employment, in order to feed and shelter his growing family, the senior Giuseppe Giovanni, at the risk of his life, had to trek to the bottom of the mountain at dawn, and at dusk, trek back up the mountain. Their main means of employment at the bottom of the mountain was the gathering and processing of olives, the gathering and processing of grapes, farming, lumber, and some cattle.

At this time, there was no law or government in the Region of Calabria. The senior Giuseppe Giovanni and all the Calabrians that had to work to live were practically enslaved to a Baron or landowner. The landowners, called padrones by the workers or peons, as previously stated, ruled the land and the peons, were not very nice about it, and paid the peons as little as possible.

LONGOBUCCO

Longobucco is in direct line from Naples, to the south, and between 1860 and 1880, because of its location, it was a very popular city for conquerors and brigands.

Calabria had many small settlements that became fiefdoms when controlled by one rich and influential man. Small wars continually broke out all over Calabria, and whoever won the war, won the fiefdom and its population. Longobucco was one such "ping pong ball" that impacted three Laurenzano brothers, living and working peacefully with their family and friends within their beloved Longobucco.

It is said that Longobucco and the surrounding areas had one of these "take possession wars" in 1877, and three Laurenzano brothers became directly involved when they fought for the side that lost the war and had to make a fast exit. Or, another story that lingers is that one of the Laurenzano brothers, after having been bitten by his padrone's favorite dog, had killed the dog dead on the spot. Since the three brothers were working together at the time of the incident, the padrone did not know which brother had killed his dog, so the padrone, owner of this very favorite, but vicious, dog, sent word that he was going to have all three brothers killed. Fact—this was not an idle threat. The padrone was sure to do as he said he would because, put simply, he was the law, and such a petty act as killing a peon, in those days, was a very common occurrence.

So, it was reasoned by the brothers that, in order for the padrone to kill them, he first had to find them, and they split up and vacated the area. One brother settled in Strongoli, located on the sea coast, north of Cotrone; another went to Verzino, in the Sili Greca Mountains; and the third went to Cutro, situated between Strongoli and Verzino, on flat farming land. Whatever the reason for taking flight from Longobucco—taking sides in a war or killing a mutt—it seemed to still be punishable by death, so they had no choice but to flee, and flee they did.

Giuseppe Giovanni Laurenzano, the oldest of the three fleeing brothers, with his life mate Teresa, big with child, and their two children in tow, arrived in the small settlement of Verzino, high in La Sili Greca Mountain Range. After arriving, they found immediate housing in a hollowed out, granite-walled cave, where ultimately, in 1878, Teresa gave birth to her third child, who they named Natale.

The family, as mentioned earlier, struggled to eke out a living. Four years later, in 1882, their last child was born to them, who they named Salvatore Pasquale. It took Giuseppe Giovanni a few years after that, but he finally moved his family from the cave to a house made of stone and plaster. Unfortunately, though, soon after the birth of their last child, Teresa, wife and mother, already had found her Lord at a very young age.

Imagine, if you will, how difficult and sorrowful Teresa's death had to be for that young, struggling family in those early years.

Caterina, their only daughter, who was about eight or nine at the time, took over the caring of the baby and the family. It is not known what happened to Caterina. For some reason, Natale did not talk of her, but I would imagine that she also passed at a young age. It is not known if the senior Giuseppe Giovanni ever remarried after the death of Teresa. The choices were very slim in Verzino, so we doubt that he ever did. In fact, the population was so slim at the time that there is no marked grave, in Verzino or anywhere else, identifying the resting place of the early Laurenzanos— Giuseppe Giovanni, Teresa, or Caterina.

How different would it have been for all the Lauranzano families if these early Laurenzanos could have spent their natural lives in Longobucco, the place of their birth? We will never know; one can only wonder.

When Natale was five years old, he was entered into the Verzino catholic school, run by the Chiesa Madre (Mother Church), as mentioned earlier, and went through the eight grades that the local pastor offered. After graduation, he worked the vineyards down the mountain for a time, as his father did, gathering and processing grapes. Later, he worked the olive grove in Verzino, gathering and processing olives. The olive grove was owned by the Leo family, and they treated Natale, as he always said, "with respect." Our relatives in Verzino said, "You would have thought he was their son, they treated him so well." Natale was a good-looking gentleman, and he soon found his way to the heart of Signore Leo's pretty daughter, Maria, who Natale courted for the next four years. When he was twenty-one (*old enough to know better*), he asked her for her hand in marriage and she accepted. On July 13, 1899, they were wed in Chiesa Madre, after which a good time was had by all in the home of the Leo family.

They were married for four years, childless, and Natale was working the Leo's olive grove in Verzino, as well as the vineyards down below the mountain, with a padrone that he hated. Since he could not go elsewhere in Italia, and wanting to make something of his life, and wanting Maria to be proud of him, he made that decision, with Maria's concurrence, to go to another country and find a new life for both of them.

After his arrival at Ellis Island, Natale struggled for two years to get a foothold in America. He often told the story of when he found himself in Pittsburgh, PA, homeless and trying to find a job and a place to settle down—he was literally starving to death. Wandering through one of the city streets, he recognized what he thought was a Verzino family name on a corner grocery store and went into the store to inquire. After several questions, back and forth, he happily discovered that the owner of the store was well acquainted with his family and friends in Verzino. The paesano fed him and let him rest, and on their invitation, Natale stayed with them for several weeks, helping the paesano with the caring of the store. It was said that the store prospered like no other time while Natale was clerking for them.

Natale's younger brother, Salvatore Pasquale sailed to America on the Prinz Adalbert, arriving at Ellis Island on May 24, 1905. Natale met him at the port of New York, and after Natale explained to him what a difficult time he was having in America, they decided that they would board another ship to Brazil, South America (S.A.), in search of relatives they believed migrated there from Longobucco. They sailed from the Port of Baltimore. The exact date of their sailing is unknown.

When they arrived together in S.A., they found work on a large coffee plantation. As Natale told the story, after about two years, he was eating lunch on this vast coffee plantation and viewed a large boa constrictor or python come down off a large tree in the adjoining jungle and swallow a cow that belonged to the plantation owner. It was after this incident, two and a half years after he first arrived in Brazil, that he decided he would return to Italy and Maria. Even though Natale and Pasquale failed to locate any relatives in Brazil who had migrated from Longobucco, Pasquale had a good job on the coffee plantation and a girl friend, so he decided to remain in S.A. He married his girl friend soon after Natale's departure.

I asked Natale one day, "Why didn't Pasquale marry his girlfriend while you were with him in S.A. so that some family would have been with him when he married?" and all he said was, "You have to know Pasquale." I had to wait many years before I discovered the meaning of that remark. I had no idea what he meant by that until my first visit to Verzino, when my cousin told me about Pasquale and what my father meant by that remark. He told me that Pasquale was not the most reliable type of person you want

6

partnering with you, but if Natale derived nothing else from his Brazil experience, he learned to speak and write Portuguese fluently.

Longobucco is the native comune for all the Laurenzanos. There was always a large amount of Laurenzanos in Longobucco up until the French occupation, around 1860, when they started leaving in large numbers. Killing and raping the citizens became commonplace. The large migration occurred between 1860 and 1870. The latest check of Laurenzanos living in Longobucco showed that the last Laurenzano left Longobucco in 1985 and settled in Rossano, where many Laurenzanos still reside, spelling their name with the infamous "e."

It is interesting to note that, at the present time, the Strongoli family members spell the name the correct way, as known in Longobucco—Laurenzano. The Verzino members—father, mother, Giuseppe, Caterina, Natale, and Pasquale, and their many offspring— spell the name Lauranzano. The members who settled in Cutra spell the name Lorenzano. Most in Italy today spell the name Laurenzano with the "e" and are settled all over Italy, America, and Argentina. We, the folks from Verzino, are the only family members who spell our name differently, other than Cutra, of course, who are off the page.

Strongoli descendants are all over the USA, originating in Brooklyn, NY. The Cutra relatives did not migrate. The Strongolese believe that they are the only Laurenzanos on earth and refuse to recognize our existence. They have a gigantic reunion every Fourth of July, where only the Strongolese are welcome.

I wonder what the senior Giuseppe would think of that, especially if he did not kill the dog.

VERZINO

Natale was the first Lauranzano born in the Comune di Verzino after the fast exit from Longobucco. He was born, literally, in a cave, as previously mentioned, that is still owned by the Lauranzano clan. Within the clan, it seems, whoever has the key owns the cave. At present, the key is held by Mesina, the widow of Cousin Natale's son Michele. (Cousin Natale is the youngest son of Natale's oldest brother). Mesina moved back to Verzino from Bari after Michele's death. The cave is presently being utilized as a storage area.

After viewing the cave and the obvious living conditions that must have prevailed at the time of the family's residence, it is no mystery to me why Natale's mother (and probably Caterina) passed away so young in age. An extra key to the cave was presented to the Beverly Lauranzanos (of Beverly, Massachusetts), so I guess we are honorary owners of the cave. I placed the key in a shadow box, along with a painted illustration of the cave. Since I did the illustration and I now have the illustration and the key, I guess I am the Beverly owner of the cave.

Back to 1907, we find Natale freshly returned from America via South America, reunited with his Maria, and very sad that he was *not* successful in America after leaving the land of his birth.

Well, in my opinion, maybe he was too young to make it without some kind of help. He had no trade or experience, and having come from such a tiny fiefdom, he did not have any friends in America, as most immigrants had when they went there searching for a better life.

Nevertheless, Natale has returned to Verzino, feeling like an utter failure, and was back helping Maria's father in their olive grove and doing odd jobs down below the mountain for the hated padrone— just as he was doing before he left for America. But once he experienced travel and had seen what could be had in America, he soon became bored and restless and decided, with Maria's agreement and participation, to return to America.

Natale's niece Maria, the daughter of his brother Giuseppe Michele, recalled her older sister Tommasina telling of the day Natale and Maria went down the mountain. She got the feeling she would never see either one ever again. She told how she cried for several days. Forty-six years later, she was very happy to see Natale again, but she never saw Maria Leo Lauranzano again. Cousin Maria was ninety-eight when she told us this story, with her younger sister Francesca, at ninety-four, nodding in agreement.

Francesca was married to Alessandro Girimonte, and Cousin Maria, Natale's niece, to Dominico Iaquinta—well known families in Verzino. Maria and Dominico married in 1910 and had one child, Salvatore, born in 1935. Francesca and Alessandro married in 1922 and had four children—Caterina in 1945, Filomena in 1947, Silvia in 1950, and Salvatore in 1960.

In the year of 1909, in October, at the age of 31, Natale landed at Ellis Island on the ship Konig Albert, out of the port of Napoli, but this time, however, with Maria at his side and with a letter from her cousin, who lived in Mansfield, Massachusetts, promising an introduction to a prospective employer. That employer was the owner of an Italian bakery in Fall River, Massachusetts.

It was many years later that I learned of this, when Maria's cousin from Mansfield told me the story. I am sorry I do not know her cousin's name because he made a very solid impact on Natale's life. But I know that Natale never forgot him and was ever grateful to him. They often corresponded and visited one another.

FALL RIVER, MASSACHUSETTS

The prospective employer in Fall River was an Italian baker by the name of Carmenuch, and true to his word   to Maria's cousin, he gave Natale an opportunity to learn a trade by giving him the promised job in his bakery. There was another man working in this bakery that was the first baker, going by the name of Raphael Marcucci, but unfortunately, he and Natale did not get along very well. The reason they did not get along was, as Natale often told the story, "I worked very hard, was very industrious, and worked many hours because I wanted very much to be a success in my new country. But Raphael saw it a different way—he thought that I was trying to take his job away, as prima panettiere."

Raphael Marcucci was also newly arrived in America, from Fondi. He was alone and found it difficult to trust anyone, having been hurt a few times and having worked hard to achieve his current position. He was also struggling to get enough money together to bring his father, mother, brother, and two sisters to America to join him from Fondi. This was quite an ambition for a young man trying to get along in a country where he could not speak or understand the language.

Years and years later, Natale and Raphael still talked of their rivalry and still argued points, like who made the best bread or who made the most money. However, it was all in fun, all in fun ...

In 1910, tragedy befell the hardworking baker, Natale. Maria took sick and went to her Lord. Can you imagine what a sad time this had to be in his life? Believe me when I tell you, he was a long time getting over her passing and grieved for a long, long period of time. After Maria's death, Natale preferred living alone. He was very lonesome and worked even harder for Carmenuch, making and delivering bread. At this time in his life, he was thinking very seriously of returning to the mountains of Calabria and Verzino. But he could not imagine life without Maria, and also, he could not imagine returning to Italia without Maria. He often thought that it was all for nothing.

Again, America was not a happy place for him. Would he ever find happiness?

It was a year or so after Maria's death that Raphael Marcucci quit the job at Carmenuch. He bought some property on Bedford Street and started his own bakery. As a result, Natale was made first baker, prima panettiere, in charge of Carmenuch's, and Raphael moved to his new location. Raphael called his new establishment The Over The Top Italian Bakery. He had a grocery store in front, a bakery in the rear, and living quarters upstairs.

It was not long after Raphael opened the new bakery and grocery store that he was successful in getting his entire immediate family to America, which included, along with his mother and father, his younger brother Guido and his two sisters, Santina and Colomba. They came to Fall River at separate times, first his Mom and Pop, then Guido, and last, on November 6 of 1912, Santina and Colomba, arriving at Ellis Island on the ship Molke. It was a proud day in Raphael's life when they all finally arrived in Fall River and were "under his roof," as he used to put it. Happiness abounded on Bedford Street, and his brother Guido started work in The Over The Top Bakery, learning the family business.

Even though The Over The Top Bakery and the store in front were thriving and Natale was now the first baker at Carmenuch's, Raphael and Natale stayed in touch, mainly because they belonged to the same Italian Social Club on Bedford Street and were drinking buddies, and also, it was strongly suspected, Raphael saw in Natale a suitable life mate for his sister, Colomba, newly arrived from Italy.

Soon after her arrival in this country, Raphael's sister Santina wed one Giovanni Giulebbe, whom she had met in Fall River. Mr. Giulebbe came to America around the same time that Santina did, but there is no record available of his migration to his new country.

Years and years later, this became a very curious matter for his family.

There was a great mystery surrounding Giovanni Giulebbe's coming to America. Since a record of his arrival is not available and much time has been expended in an attempt to locate these records, it has been suspected that he came here under a different name. For some reason, we think the original name was Lombardo and that, for some reason, he found it necessary to change his name to Giulebbe. His daughter Lena suspected this until the day she died, and before her death, she often discussed her efforts to conclude the mystery of her true family name.

But the family name is Giulebbe, and since we cannot prove otherwise, that is the name we will use.

Colomba Marcucci and Natale Lauranzano (the handsome widower) met in the spring of 1913. Raphael introduced his sister to the hardworking and lonesome Natale one Sunday afternoon at a special function given at the Italian Social Club. They got along well together and saw each other as often as was possible. This did not prove often enough for the two lovebirds, so Natale took a rental room on the third floor of Raphael's new place on Bedford Street. This move enabled him to see his future bride more often. A few months later, Natale proposed and Colomba accepted, and their futures looked bright and secure.

Natale was starting to think that America, after all, might truly be the land of opportunity, and maybe, just maybe, he could still realize some happiness.

Natale Lauranzano was now thirty-four years old, no spring chicken, and he was childless from his first marriage, but he was a very strong man—not very tall, maybe five foot nine inches, but built very heavy in the chest area. He was a handsome man. He always had a moustache, the handlebar type, when such things were popular. He used to wax the ends and curl them up, up, and away. A devil was he. A favorite with all the women, but no time to do any womanizing because of his heavy work schedule and being true to Maria's memory. Although his responsibilities in the bakery took all of his time, this did not discourage the ladies from visiting the bakery to say hello to that handsome baker. Many times, Colomba told us of her jealousy and her watchful eye on her suitor.

But, not to worry, work came first. After the suffering of his first visit to America, Natale knew the proper values, and now, he had Colomba.

It was later rumored that the real reason Raphael started his own bakery was that Natale had outworked him so badly that Carmenuch was going to promote Natale to the first baker's position and demote Raphael. Many an argument ensued between the two men because of that rumor, and Colomba was always in the middle of their arguments, never knowing whose side to take. But Colomba was accustomed to her brother's bravado because she was a Marcucci too, and she knew a Marcucci was never afraid to voice an opinion, so she sort of sympathized with the man she was going to marry.

It was proven in later years and experienced, many times, by her children that she, too, could voice some powerful arguments.

Well, it proved to be a moot point, because Raphael quit Carmenuch before the rumored demotion, opened his own bakery, and got himself married. His marriage occurred in 1913. And not to be outdone, Natale proposed to Colomba. She accepted his proposal, and history was made. Raphael was happy, Natale was happy, and of course, Colomba was out of this world with delight—after all, didn't she capture the heart of a very desirable man?

To Raphael's credit, however, all he ever seemed to want in his life was for his Mom, Pop, and sibs to be happy, no matter what the cost.

Colomba was a tallish girl, taller than her fiancée. She was shy, mainly because her only language was Italian and she was unaccustomed to the American way. After all, she was only in America a little over a year. She was ten years younger than Natale and became very devoted to the gentleman, even more than to her beloved brothers (barely). She loved her brothers dearly, but she loved Natale even more. She would eventually spend forty-two years as Natale's life mate and the loving mother of ten children. Raphael had planned it right. His sister would marry Natale Lauranzano, a good father, a good man, and a good provider.

Natale finally hit it right in America, even though he experienced a great loss when his beloved childhood sweetheart and mate, Maria, passed away. He would be happy with his second wife, Colomba, though, even though he loved her dearly, he went through life constantly missing Maria. Her death broke his heart. In future years, he never failed to visit Maria's gravesite whenever he returned to Fall River, and he always stayed in touch with Maria's family.

No 106 The wedding picture of Colomba (Marcucci) and Natale Lauranzano, my mother and father, who were married in 1912 in St Anne's Church in Fall River, Mass. The reception was held at the home of Raphael Marcucci on Bedford Street, brother of the bride.

THE NUPTIALS

On a warm and sunny Sunday afternoon in 1913, in their newly adopted city of Fall River, Massachusetts, Ms. Colomba Marcucci of Fondi, Italy, took, as her loving husband and life partner, Mr. Natale Lauranzano, of Verzino, Italy.

... and life started for all of us, as we know it, in America.

Faust and Maria Fiore, friends for many years, stood for the newly wedded couple as they recited their vows at St. Anne's, on Bedford Street. Many friends and family were present at the church and at the reception. The reception was held at Mr. Raphael Marcucci's home, brother of the bride, where all the guests wished the newlyweds well, and a good time was had by all. *Hooray!!*

There was no honeymoon. Early Monday, like four in the morning, Natale reported to work at the bakery. The bread had to get out, and Natale was the first baker. He ran the bakery and was vital to the well being of the business. Natale and his bride lived with Raphael and his bride on top of the bakery on Bedford Street. It was a three-floor structure. In between the two businesses—the store in front and the bakery in the rear—Raphael maintained a small living quarters, with a kitchen and a nap couch, which is very convenient for people who work from dawn to dusk. The second floor was a regular apartment, with three bedrooms, kitchen, living room, and dining room. Natale and Colo (as Colomba was called) lived in these quarters.

Unlike Maria, Colomba blessed Natale with children ... I mean, plenty of children. First, on March 1, 1913, came Maria, a very beautiful baby. Colomba often said, "Everyone adored mia Maria. She was un belle bambina." (And, is it not a credit to Colomba that she would agree to name her first girl baby Maria?) Almost simultaneously, however, Raphael's wife also had a baby girl, who was named

Concetta. Living in the same house, they were almost one, shuttling between the two mothers.

In 1915, Colomba had another girl named Gennina. She was also adorable, but Colomba was really starting to test herself, minding two children—and most of the time three, when adding Concetta to the formula—and also working in the store and bakery. Raphael's wife was not as strong anymore, and Colomba had to take on double duty by taking over the care of Concetta. Mrs. Marcucci then gave birth to a boy, who they named Giuseppe. Now, Colomba had four to take care of.

But why stop there? It was soon after, on May 9, 1917, when Mr. and Mrs. Natale Lauranzano announced the birth of a girl baby named Yolanda. Now, there were five for Colomba to tend to, since her sister-in-law was now even weaker. And then, again—I know this is hard to believe, but it is true nonetheless—once more, and almost simultaneously with Yolanda, another baby boy was born to Mrs. Marcucci, and they named the little boy Tomasino. And now there were six little ones for Colomba to care for.

But Colomba was strong and her sister-in-law was getting even weaker and could not tend to her children at all. Actually, if the truth be known, she was deathly ill, and everyone was very, very worried for her. At this point in time, all the children referred to Colo as Mama, and still Colo had to labor in her brother's bakery and store and see to the needs of all six children. Colo did this for about five long years and never complained (so they say).

But, I'll bet there were many times she wished she had never left Fondi.

The expected sad day in the home of Raphael Marcucci arrived, when his beloved wife went to her Lord in 1917. This occurred soon after the birth of Tomasino, when she contracted influenza, and with her weakened condition, she could not survive. Colo took over Raphael's household completely. Her new husband, Natale, was going to his job at daybreak or earlier and coming home at dusk or later. I guess Colo was doing the same, but did not leave her brother's property to do it.

Late in 1917, within his job description with Carmenuch, Natale delivered bread to Newport, RI, and while there one day, he saw an opportunity to purchase an old building on Thames Street and thought it would be a good place to start his own bakery. He took the plunge. He purchased the building, quit his job with Carmenuch, and moved to Newport, determined and alone, leaving Colomba in Fall River to care for the six children. Colomba refused to join her husband in Newport, RI because of her loyalty to Raphael and his brood of three.

Someone had to do it, and she did.

Early in 1918, Raphael started seeing another woman in a very serious way. She was a recent arrival from Italy, and her name was Giuseppina. After a short courtship and the obvious dire need to wed, they married in late 1918. Colomba turned Concetta, Giuseppe, and Tomasino over to her care, packed up her own Maria, Gennina, and Yolanda, and hopped a bus to Newport and her new adventure. Raphael's brood of three, left behind in Fall River, had a hard time getting adjusted to their new mama. They missed Colomba, and cried endlessly for the woman they regarded as their own.

I might add that, even when grown and with their own families, they remembered Zia Colo as their lost mama. They never lost their love for her. Well... they did eventually.

As Natale and Colomba worked hard to establish their new bakery in a new city, they learned that Colo's sister, Santina, and her man, Giovanni Giulebbe, had uprooted from Fall River and relocated to Beverly, Massachusetts. Having also worked in Carmenuch's bakery, Giovanni had the necessary experience to bake Italian bread, so that he was able to get himself situated with Titoni's Italian Bakery in Beverly. Titoni's was located on the corner of Chestnut and Rantoul. An automobile dealership was also located there for years.

When she moved to Beverly, Santina was also caring for a brood of three. Perina came first, a little before our Maria; then Lena, a little before Gennina; and then Alfredo, a little before Yolanda. When Santina and Giovanni were relocating, Santina was carrying Gennaro, her youngest and last child, who was born simultaneously with our Giuseppe. So the kids were coming fast and furious to all the Marcuccis, with the exception of their handsome brother Guido, who was the youngest and not married yet, but who was thinking seriously of doing so. He was keeping steady company with Theresa Fiore, a young, pretty, and debonair Fall River girl from a well known Italian/American family.

Guido was still working for his brother Raphael in The Over The Top Bakery and was doing well. His brother was paying him well enough to actually be considered as a partner—pay wise, anyhow. So, in 1918, Guido actually did it, he tied the knot. They were married at St. Anne's in Fall River. A gala reception was held at the Italian Social Club on Bedford Street. His brother was his best man, and Theresa's sister, her maid of honor. Natale and Colomba Lauranzano of Newport, RI, Colomba being sister of the groom, attended with all three of their children in tow.

Meanwhile, on the island in Narragansett Bay, Natale and Colomba were still at it. Colomba gave birth to Giuseppe in 1919, and in 1922, gave birth to Natale Jr. The bakery was doing just okay. Natale was not happy with the location because Newport did not have enough Italian people to eat his bread. Yet, he was still working the bakery by himself, and working twelve to fourteen hours every day, including Sundays.

So when did he have the time to make babies?

For two years, Natale worked alone, making and delivering the bread, and then, one day, he got a letter from his brother-in-law Giovanni Giulebbe. The letter changed all our lives (*oh, and by the way, Colomba is carrying again.*) The letter advised Natale that Beverly, Massachusetts, was crying for an Italian bakery. There was but one, and Mr. Titoni was reluctant to stay in the business, and Beverly had a large Italian population and could support two bakeries. And Santina missed her sister. Would Natale consider moving to Beverly to start a bakery? Giovanni promised to help him. "Beverly is crying for him," Giovanni said.

Well, Natale took a weekend and a day to visit Beverly and the Giulebbes. Colomba's brother Guido took care of the business in Newport while Natale was on his exploration. He liked what he saw in Beverly and decided almost immediately to make the move. On his return to Newport, he gave the bakery to Guido outright, who was delighted. Guido moved to Newport and took over the bakery. He and Theresa had two children at the time, Victor and Ester, and during their first year in Newport, Hecter was born to them. They soon had another boy after Hecter, who did not make it out of the hospital. Their last child, Credo, came much later. As I previously stated, the Marcuccis are very productive people and hardworking.

Guido and Teresa became successful in Newport. They soon upgraded to new quarters, down Thames Street, a little way from the old place. It was a three-story affair, on a corner, with the bakery in the back of the first floor and, like his older brother in Fall River, he opened a store in the front part of the building. Their living quarters were situated on the second floor. In the back of the building, on the side street, there was a garage for their delivery truck and family sedan. The end of the short, dead-end side street emptied into the bay. Natale's original building was taken over by the city and torn down, where they erected a city water pump station. Guido prospered and raised his family, wanting for nothing.

BEVERLY, MASSACHUSETTS

Meanwhile back in Beverly, Massachusetts, Natale and his brood of five and a half were looking for a place to settle. First, they found an apartment on Federal Street, in back of the Gloria Chain store. At that time, the Gloria Chain store was on the first floor of a three story tenement house on the corner. They did not stay there long. Natale found a house and a place to make bread behind the Dreamland Café on Rantoul Street. This place proved very difficult on everybody, which obliged Natale to strike a deal with Mr. Titoni to make bread in his shop and sell it where he could. Again, this was very difficult on both families, and Mr. Titoni, especially, was becoming a bit agitated. It was during these problem days with Mr. Titoni that Natale bought a house and an adjacent vacant corner lot on West Dane and Chase Streets, just down from Rantoul Street, smack in the middle of the Italian district and Ward Three.

In the course of selling bread in Beverly, Natale made many friends. One such friend was Pasquale Incampo, a very talented mason who practiced his trade in Beverly for many years. Frank Allaruzzo, who owned a home on Chase Street, near the bakery, worked for Incampo for many years and was also an ace mason. Many lasting and beautiful brick-and-cement structures were constructed in Beverly by Incampo and Allaruzzo, particularly after the war, when they constructed the best front steps in all of the North Shore area. Many veterans moving into their new, post-war homes restructured their steps just to have Incampo and/or Allaruzzo do the work. They were always much in demand.

I remember that Mr. Incampo used to buy one round loaf of bread every day for many years. At one point, for a while, Pasquale Incampo was the only customer that wanted a round loaf of bread, but Natale made it for him anyway.

Pasquale and Natale discussed for some time, day in and day out, the construction of the new building on the vacant lot that was adjacent to the house, which was presently strewn with tall grass, weeds, old plants, and old and abused fruit trees. In early 1923, they came to an agreement on price and put the building plan together, and construction began.

The unexpected always happens. Early one morning, about this time in Natale's life, Mr. Titoni got into a very serious accident in his bakery. They believe he caught his arm in the mixing machine in a very serious way, and it eventually caused his death. Natale continued making his bread there for his own customers, and he also worked Titoni's clientele. He had to put off the construction of his bakery until Titoni's business could be liquidated. Titoni's children knew nothing of the business and wanted no part of it. It took about two months to close up Titoni's, and for Natale, it was two months of misery. The two men grew to be very fond of one another, but there was no way that Titoni could stay open. Natale was too far into his own bakery. Mrs. Titoni understood this and accepted that, when Natale's new bakery was complete, they would shut down Titoni's.

This whole episode was a shock to the Titoni family. They lost their father and husband and had to close their business very suddenly. The Titoni family consisted of an oldest girl, who married John Carbone, who lived on top of the Carbone family store on the corner of Rantoul and Bow, across from the Ford dealership. John Carbone later opened a restaurant in the same building. Then, there was Bernie, who married Virginia Gia Carnevale; and Rudy, the youngest.

Bernie, Gia, and Rudy moved to Texas several years later, and were never seen in Beverly again, as far as I know.

Six months after Titoni's death, Natale bought much of the Titoni bakery equipment and moved it all to West Dane Street. Mrs. Titoni moved in with her daughter, made a life for herself, and lived for many years, remaining good friends with Natale and Colo. The Titonis were an important part of Natale's life. They were essential in getting him started with his own business in Beverly.

I strongly feel that Mr. Titoni and Natale Lauranzano would have been business partners had Mr. Titoni lived. He and Mr. Titoni grew very close. Natale was never sorry he made the move from Newport to Beverly.

On May 18, 1923, a boy was born to Natale and Colomba— their sixth child, that they named Americo, proud to be an American, and he was the first born in their new home on West Dane Street in Beverly. A midwife was utilized to bring Americo into the world. Her name was Maria Masarella, but she was called

"Mariamala" by all the Italians in the neighborhood. The nickname means "Mary, the sick." She lived alone on Park Street. Her place is still there, beside the city stables. It has a vacant store in the front that Mariamala use to run. There actually was another two-and-a-half-story home between her and the city stables, where the DiRubio family lived. The city took the DiRubio homestead when it expanded the stables. John DiRubio, one of the sons, was probably the greatest athlete to ever live in Beverly, and he later worked for Natale. But that is another story for another time.

Now for the big news—I am Americo, and I am writing this story, and now I am a part of the planet and can refer to Natale as Pa and Colomba as Ma.

Let me tell you, I always knew that Mariamala brought me into the world, and all during my youth, I use to stare at her in awe. Later in life, I delivered bread to her, and you would think I was delivering bread to God. She laughed because she knew what was on my mind. She dressed peculiarly, always wearing sneakers and with a broken-down hem, and used to roam the city mumbling. What she was mumbling, no one knew. Probably mumbling that she should have strangled me with the umbilical cord at birth. But she came from a well respected Beverly family, and Ma used to say she was "smart as a whip."

See, I am calling Colomba "Ma." Ma was introduced to Mariamala by Ma's sister, Zia Santina. Boy, it's great to be born and be part of a family. Now, Santina is my zia (aunt), and I also have five siblings of my very own. So far, life is great, and I was just born a little while ago—and I have my very own midwife!

The house we all moved into at 36 West Dane Street, before my birth, was two and a half stories, with clapboard siding, what there was of them. Much of the clapboard was loose or falling off, and what was there needed painting. At the front of the house there was an open front porch, or veranda, that abutted the sidewalk. All the windows rattled and would not open. The interior was a nightmare, and my sisters never got tired of describing it, in their words, as "filthy dirty and vermin populated." My sisters, stubbornly, would not enter the abode until my father cleaned it up a little. It got in this condition because an elderly lady lived there for quite some years and could not manage much in the way of cleaning.

The back of the house had about twenty feet or so of backyard before abutting the property of the Papa family, our neighbor for the next umpteen years. It seemed that the yard was once gardened because there was evidence of some old corn stalks here and there. There was also evidence of an outhouse shed that, thankfully, was not in use. At the side of the house, towards Chase Street, there was the vacant lot, with evidence of gardening and fruit trees, and of neglect. This was the location of the future home of the Columbus Bakery, our family business.

I wonder if the name had anything to do with the Columbus Park in Fall River, where Pa's first wife, Maria, and Pa spent time together.

Pa was a very handy fixer upper, or he soon learned to be, with all the repairs that had to be done to the house. The house had no central heating, so the first thing on his list of repairs was to install a new furnace. Stevens, the only black family in Beverly, did the work for us. Of course, I did not mind the cold mornings before the furnace was put in, getting out of bed into a cold, cold room and going to school in the cold, cold weather, because I was nice and snug in my Mama's belly and enjoying the ride. I even got my Mama out of a lot of work. But the month of May came around all too fast, and the easy ride ended. After Pa got everyone comfortable in the new house, he got Pasquale Incampo and the Incampo crew, and they started pouring the cement and giving birth to our new bakery. A lot of cement was poured—the entire bakery floor, the yard between the house and bakery, and the entire heated, two-car garage, where Pa would keep his bread truck and the Buick Roadster he would soon own.

In 1923, the new Columbus Bakery opened for business. Pa was the first baker and Giovanni Giulebbe was his assistant (and brother-in-law). You would have thought he would now be looking for people willing to eat his bread, but that was not the case. With the Titoni Bakery out of the business, he had customers clamoring for his Italian bread, exactly as Giovanni Giulebbe had predicted in the famous letter to Pa. There was a pretty fair population of Italian/Americans in Beverly who made their living from employment with the United Shoe Machinery Corporation, which held the monopoly on all shoe machinery throughout the world. The Italian/American neighborhood was basically Ward Three, from Elliot Street to Bow Street and from Cabot Street to Park Street. Natale started immediately with three mixes a day, and he sold every loaf.

We were now, truly, a family of means, property owners, and true Republicans.

The girls had started at the Washington School, as soon as they arrived in Beverly. Mary was ten; Gennina, now called Jenny, was eight; and Yolanda, now called Allie, was six. Life was great for them. They went to school, played all afternoon—hop scotch, jump rope—and Ma even allowed them ten cents a piece to go to the movies on Saturday, plus one penny for candy. Clara Bow and Janet Gaynor became their favorites. Pepina Minutello's candy store, across from the Washington School, on the corner of Roundy and Chase, was their favorite place to visit if they had a penny. and Ma always saw that they had one. Life was a ball for the top three.

As for the boys, Giuseppe, now formerly called Joseph, with the nickname of Joe, was four going on five and was the scourge of the neighborhood. Discipline was his middle name. Then there was Natale Jr., later called Ned—he was almost two and was under the strict control of Allie. Ma was taking personal care of yours truly, the newly born Americo, later to be dubbed, Mareeko, Merico, or Rico. What a blast I was having. I was being handed to and fro among Ma's neighborhood friends, from Vincenza Papa, to Rosaria Nardella, to Susan Carnevale, to Alvira DiPoalo, to Eraina Ramare. They could not resist me, I was one cute little guy.

Short lived, however, because one even cuter would soon arrive, and her name would be Francesca—we will call her Fannie—and she would be number seven. Oh, joy. True to my word, along came Francesca, called Fannie. Will Ma and Pa ever stop?

More on Fannie later. I was now three years old. Like I said previously, Joe's middle name should have been discipline, because he was always on the go, and Pa was always trying to catch up to him. Much to Ma's chagrin, I was always chasing after Joe, too, trying to catch up to my big brother. One cute Saturday morning, I was following Joe while Joe was scurrying away from our abode with his friends. Joe and his friends crossed Rantoul Street and I followed close behind. Joe tried to chase me away many times before crossing Rantoul, but I paid no attention to him. Well, folks, I never made it to the other side. A car hit me and I was rushed to the Beverly Hospital, where I stayed for three months with a broken leg, and I was only three years old.

While I was in the hospital, you just would not believe it, I cried endlessly, until I spied one of my sisters or my mother through my window, coming up the entrance stairs with a paper bag in their hand. Knowing the paper bag contained my beloved vanilla ice cream, I would stop my endless crying and dutifully await my treat.

I remember my nurse's name was Polly, and I know she despised me because of my three months of endless crying. Curiously, to this day, my favorite ice cream flavor is vanilla, I wonder why?

I do think, though, that Pa is still giving Joe a hard time in heaven over that slip in responsibility. I can hear Joe saying, "Pa, this is heaven, give me a break."

I remember being in the children's ward, located in the old hospital buildings, the two buildings nearest to the street, with the white porches and columns. That was where the entrance to the hospital was. The hospital was located on the outskirts of Beverly. Nothing was around the hospital but trees. Even the high school, that is now Briscoe Middle School, was not there yet. That was three years away in 1929. Johnnie DiRubio would be the captain of the first football team at the new high school. Beverly, at the time, was populated with about 15,000 people. Gloucester Crossing still had a manually operated barrier raising and lowering the railroad gates. It was truly a garden city then.

Fannie is now about one and growing fast. Ma is caring for her, and Allie now has Ned and Rico added to her string of home duties. Allie is now ten going on thirty and sort of delegated by Ma as her assistant. Did Allie campaign for or even desire this enviable position? I really do not think so, but Mary and Jenny were busy playing, and I guess Ma did not want to disturb them. However, I think that Ma preferred Allie because Allie was more compassionate and loving, but as disciplinarians go, I would have preferred that Ma watched over us.

But one can not have everything, especially when you're a little kid and no one listens to you, anyhow.

As it turned out for Allie, she went through life unmarried and childless, but she had more experience at bringing up children than a majority of women that were married for years and had their own children. Allie filled in for Ma in the care of the household, caring for Ned, me, Fannie, and the three others that would come later. She cooked, cleaned, gave baths, and went to school and/or worked her outside job, and she still showered us with love and devotion. She had to make many sacrifices and, like Ma, she did it without complaint. And God knows, she had much to complain about. We were not easy kids to watch over. In fact, we were very difficult kids to watch over. But Allie was very devoted to Ma and was always helping Ma see to our comfort and to the running of the house.

Often, Ma had her hands full helping Pa in the bakery, and there was only twenty-four hours in a day. It turned out that, unknown to Pa at the time that he hired him, Giovanni was not the most reliable employee one could have working for you. In fact, he was far from it. Turned out, he was absent from work more times then not. At daybreak, when you expect someone at work to mix the bread dough and he does not show, it is difficult to get a replacement at such an early hour. Ma, of course, was called to the rescue, and true to form, she was always there to help where she was needed. Of course, she also helped her sister Santina by saving Giovanni's job, for even though Pa wanted to let him go many times, Ma would never allow it. So, she often did Giovanni's work for him and would not allow Pa to even dock his pay. Did Giovanni, now called John, appreciate this kindness? It's hard to say... but it didn't seem so.

The Marcuccis sure stuck together, right Pa?

Allie is starting the sixth grade, Joe is starting the fourth grade, Ned is starting the second grade, and Americo (that's me) is starting the first grade. Ma delegates her chosen assistant, Allie, to accompany me to school and register me into the first grade. Allie never liked the name Americo, even though she professed her patriotism. She preferred the name Enrico because of the then-very-popular singer from Italy, Enrico Caruso. When the principal, Miss Driver, asked for my name, Allie announced it to be Enrico, and Enrico it has been ever since.

One thing I know, Allie has always liked opera music, you got to give her that. And when I think about it, so did Ma. I wonder if they ...

Six of us are now in school, and Fannie has two more years to go before starting. When Allie takes Fanny to school, I hope Allie keeps Fannie's name intact. When Fannie was four, she had a little mishap before she started school. One evening at about six o'clock, I believe it was the Fourth of July, she had a nickel and she wanted to buy some sparklers from Ricci's Market, across Rantoul Street. Always an independent thinker, she ventured this trip solo, and never made it to the other side of Rantoul Street. You guessed it, a car hit poor Fannie, and a bunch of guys hanging on the corner of Rantoul and West Dane carried her home, entering through the front door. (*Was this to be a family trait?*)

You never heard so much crying or saw so much blood. I was relaxing on the front porch at the time, lying on the wicker sofa, and I saw the whole thing. She was rushed to the hospital, and there she stayed, also for three months, and also with a broken leg, and also looking out the window for her sisters or for Ma, carrying a brown paper bag containing vanilla ice cream from Macauley's Drug Store on Gloucester Crossing.

And, you know what? Sister Fran's favorite is vanilla, too. Makes you wonder, does it not?

VERZINO, ITALY

With Fannie recuperating in the hospital, we visit Verzino again to look into the life of Giuseppe Michele, the current patriarch of Verzino's Lauranzano family, Pa's older brother. Giuseppe Michele continued their father's legacy in Verzino, as they know it there today. He spent his entire life in this tiny settlement and never had the urge to leave. Whenever Pa suggested that his brother might want to live in America, he would vehemently refuse. Pa wrote him many letters, some requesting he come to America, but Pa would always end up saying that his brother refused his offer again. I think Pa missed having family here with him.

Giuseppe Michele Lauranzano married Filomena Astorino circa 1895 in Verzino, and they enjoyed a harsh but happy life together. They had many difficult times in the isolation of Verzino and in the rearing of their children, but at the end, they managed to put it all together. We know this because the family that Michele and Filomena left behind is one that they, *and all of us*, can truly be proud of. The offspring that Giuseppe and Filomena were blessed with were:

Tommasina, born in 1898, who married Luigi Tallarico.
>They brought two sons into the world:
>Dominico, born 1922
>Giuseppe, born 1924

Giovanni, born in 1908, never married, died in 1934 at the age of 26. Maria, born in 1910, married Dominico Iaquinta.
>They brought one son into the world:
>Salvatore, born in 1935

Francesca, born in 1916, married Alessandro Girimonte.
>They brought into the world:
>Caterina, born 1945 Filomena, born 1947 Silvia, born 1950

Salvatore, born in 1960, who has a law practice with an office in Crotone and Verzino

Cousin Natale, born in 1922, married Luigina Clausi.

(This is Franco's father and mother.)

They brought into the world.

Michele, born 1942 Filomena, born 1945 Carolina, born 1948 Francesco, born 1951

I recall Pa going back to Verzino with son Joe, the oldest boy child. They went by ship, and Joe had his new, blue Oldsmobile shipped over there on the same ship. Joe was going to drop Pa off in Verzino and then tour Italia and Europa for three months. This he did, and Pa went back to his roots. *But, that is a story for another time.*

In the year 1910, when Pa's first wife Maria's father died in Verzino, the family's olive grove had passed on to her, back in Fall River. (Later, when Maria died, the olive grove went to her spouse, Pa.) Pa was busy in Fall River, and since he was not inclined to return to Verzino to work the olive grove, he had given the running of the grove and the benefits thereof to his older brother, Giuseppe Michele. Upon Michele's death, Pa then turned it over to Cousin Natale, his namesake nephew, youngest son of Giuseppe Michele. Now, much later, during this visit there with oldest son Joe, Pa *legally* turned the groves ownership over to his nephew, who later, upon his retirement, turned the grove over to his sole surviving son, Francesco.

At present, Francesco operates the grove and the processing of the olives into virgin oil. This processing is all done in Verzino, in another cave-like structure dug into the granite wall of the Sili Greca mountainside. This olive grove has been active for well over a hundred years, and Francesco is keeping it alive by the hiring of outside professionals to do the heavy lifting. Formerly, Francesco would personally return to Verzino from Bari every year to supervise the work, but at present, his job in Bari takes up all of his time.

When Giuseppe Michele and his offspring were dominant in Verzino, the life was harsh because, at most, it was a forgotten little fiefdom, once owned entirely by one man, in the large and awesome Province of Contanzaro. Contanzaro had so many little burgs within its domain that they literally did not know Verzino existed. As a result, Verzino's inhabitants had to live with dirt roads, unattended sanitation needs, unattended water supply, and uncollected trash, and with many more failed services. When you question Contanzaro's humanitarian interests, you get to understand that, during those early years, there were many, many more responsibilities than they had funds for.

The Lauranzano clan and the other prominent families of Verzino had nowhere to turn but to themselves, and somehow, they got through it and survived. They tended to their kitchen gardens, in small plots in and around Verzino. Together, they raised farm animals, chicken, turkey, pig, and goat and made their own cheese. Their dinner tables consisted only of food grown or produced by them in their kitchen gardens, orchids, or livestock.

There is little wonder, in my mind, that we had such a difficult time in dissuading the Italians, after World War II, from voting pro-communism.

Pa and Allie received letters from Giuseppe Michele early on, and later, from his son Natale and, after the war, from Filomena and/or Natale, requesting help with clothes for the young ones. My clothes used to disappear so often, I really worried that spirits existed in the house on West Dane Street. When I discovered where my clothes went, I knew that Verzino's Lauranzano kids dressed better than I or my brothers did.

Allie was making a career out of the slogan, "Clothes for Verzino."

During the war, I used to think that our relatives in Verzino lived so far from humanity, in such an inconsequential mountain area, that they probably did not know a war was going on. It was not until my first visit there that I discovered that my cousin Natale served in the Italian army. His daughter Filomena showed me a picture of him in an Italian army uniform, jokingly aiming a rifle. He was stationed in Africa.

When looking at the picture, I had to wonder if, given the chance, he would have aimed that rifle at me, when he suddenly told us, as though he read my mind, "When I was in Africa, I thought a lot about my American cousins, and I never, never aimed a weapon in the direction of the Americans, for fear that …"

BEVERLY, MASSACHUSETTS

Our new home in Beverly Massachusetts at 36 West Dane Street was bursting with pride and excitement. We were still new in this city, and Pa and Ma were making big strides towards a successful stay. Fanny was the last blessing bestowed on Ma, and she was aflutter with her presence, while Allie, her chosen second in command, kept the rest of the young ones in their proper place. No one envied Allie's job, but I think Allie truly loved us and loved looking out for us.

It was mid-1925, and the bakery, now officially named Columbus Bakery and operating somewhat smoothly, was doing three mixes a day and serving the good people of Beverly and the surrounding area. Pa was thinking seriously about adding a grocery store on the front side of the bakery, abutting the sidewalk,

(just like his brother-in-laws in Fall River and Newport).

It is unbelievable that Pa didn't have enough worries operating the bakery. He started construction on the store, dividing the bakery almost in half by placing a wall down the near center. Then, he got a carpenter to put in a hardwood floor, in the store section only, and added large store windows in the front and on the Chase Street side to display merchandise. He put in an ice chest, counter, and scale; installed a door on the corner; and bought some merchandise to sell, and he was ready to open for business. All he required was someone to manage and tend to the store.

Because I knew my Pa so very well, I am now imagining what he was "sleeping on" during that period. "Lets see now. Colo has some free time, but she has a language problem. Hmm, lets see now, Maria is ten going on eleven, and she gets home from school about three o'clock ....

I am happy to report, they both won out—Ma opened the store in the morning and Maria relieved her after school—and this is how Maria, later known as Mary, became an expert store manager and Pa, an expert in human resources. He had a unique way of recruiting personnel—he grew his own short list.

My having recently been in the hospital with a broken leg, you would think, would make my oldest sister, now the assistant manager of Pa's new store, a soft touch for me to wangle a Hostess Cupcake or two, now and then. No way—she took her job too seriously. You couldn't squeeze a loose Cheese T Bit from her. Mary grew up in Pa's store, and it turned out to be her specialty. And several years later, it was in this store that she met her future husband. He delivered ice for Kelleher's Ice and Coal Company, located on Park Street, and serviced Pa's store. *With ice! Okay?*

In the meantime, Ma was at it again, with another boy, Uncle Raphael's namesake, becoming the newest kid on the block. Ma tended to Raphael's needs, as she did for all the others. Her daily schedule went something like this:

Out of bed at four.
Change and feed Ralph.
Take Ralph in the bakery with her.
Help Pa weigh the dough into loaves.
Return to the house.
Get the top four out of bed. Get them ready for school.
Get the bottom three up and dressed.
Feed them all breakfast.
Bring the bottom four to the bakery.
Help Pa with the "bastoon" (shape the dough).
Open the store.
Help Pa put the bread dough into the oven.
It starts all over with a new batch of dough and the kids.

Pa bought a car. *Why? Ma told him to, that's why.* It was a Buick Roadster, dark green, with a black canvas convertible top. Ma thought that it was time for us to visit her brothers. Both her brothers had their own cars and visited us occasionally, with their families in tow, and Ma wanted the same for us. I remember our first trip to Fall River in our new vehicle It was a trip from hell. First, you have to remember Pa hadn't been driving too long, and he hadn't driven any long distances. Believe me, Beverly to Fall River was a long distance, considering the route you had to take.

You drove through Salem, up Highland Avenue, West Lynn, over the Chelsea bridge, through Copley Square, down Tremont Street, into Columbus Avenue to Roxbury and Route 138, and on and on and on. We would start the trip at four in the morning and get there sometime late morning, with Ma and Pa in the front seat and Raphael on Mom's lap, the bottom four in the pullout seats, and the top three, comfortably, in the rear seat. Allie would always give me a whack across the back of my head every now and then, for no apparent reason. *I think she loved me best.*

Late in 1928, Ma started showing again, and the bottom four started wondering who was going to join us in this mad race to become what we thought was the largest family on the face of the earth. In this time period, Pa sold the canvas top Buick and bought another Buick, but this time, a sedan, green and big, with pullout seats. He parked it in the heated garage in the right-hand stall. What a beautiful sight that was. I took my naps in the back seat while it sat in the garage. *It was so comfortable, and the upholstery smelled s-o-o-o good. We were truly on our way to becoming true Republicans.*

In May of 1929, out came Uncle Guido's namesake. Yes, another boy, and he was named Guido. We all agreed that he was a cute thing. He possessed blond hair, with light complexion, and he was forever crying. As cute as he was, he was still a pain in the neck to most of us with that infernal crying. But let me tell you this, we witnessed an immediate love for this baby, never seen before in the annals of babyhood. Allie took to little Guido like she took to no other. She immediately claimed this little one for her own. She cared for him when he was ill, which was often. She claimed as her own the right to dress him. But she had to let Ma feed him, only until he was old enough to be fed from the table. And so it went. We didn't mind as long as we got *some* attention. You have to give that to Allie. As much as she loved little Guido? She gave the rest of us just as much care. *Now we were nine, four girls (ugh) and five boys. (Hooray! We outnumber them.)*

To recap the "math," with the first American generation of the Lauranzano family, we have the following established:

Maria (Mary), age 16 store assistant manager
Gennina (Jenny), age 14 in training, accountant Yolanda (Allie), age 12 assistant home care giver
Giuseppe (Joe), age 10 assistant baker Natale Jr. (Ned), age 8 assistant baker Enrico (Marico), age 7 assistant in sales Francesca (Fanny), age 5 unemployed Raphael (Luffy), age 3 unemployed Guido (Buddy) age 1 unemployed
Another on the way Ma is showing (*What a surprise!*)

There had to be something in the air around our neighborhood—all the wives were having babies during the same year that we opened our bakery on West Dane Street. A lot of our neighbors were from Italia and were raising families. For instance, I started school with Gloria, from next door. We walked to school every day together. Her mother was a Pinciaro. Then there was Nicky Papa, Freddie Pinciaro, Frankie Consoli, Billie Scotti, Jimmie DiPaolo, Gino Pasquarelli, Vincent Bussone,

Margaret Onesta, Stephan Petrosino, Stevie Fortunato, Joe Detorre, Mary Detorre, and, oops, Eric Willis—I mention him because he used to do my homework every day. He lived on Mulberry Street and was Bobby Tate's cousin.

All the above were born the same year, within a couple of blocks of one another. This is neighborhood planning at its best ... or the baby boom of 1923 ... or, was God making sure we had the necessary personnel to win a war that was coming up in eighteen or so years.

AN UNEXPECTED VISITOR

In the late twenties, on a quiet Saturday afternoon, Pa received a call from his younger brother Pasquale, who lived in Brazil, informing us that he was in Boston, in the South Station, and needed a ride to Beverly. This was out of the blue, completely unexpected. Naturally, Pa gassed up the Buick, and with Joe and Mary at his side, they journeyed to Boston to bring Pasquale to Beverly. They left Beverly approximately four in the afternoon and arrived back in Beverly at almost midnight. When they got in, they were very tired. Ma had a bed made up in the sun parlor, and they put Uncle Pasquale away for the night.

Sunday morn, Ma had a big breakfast waiting for her brother-in-law, and there was a big welcome by everyone. Our uncle was dazzled by all the kids that kept coming downstairs, Mary through Fanny, seven at the moment. After all the hugs and kisses, Pasquale announced to Pa that he wanted to stay in America and bring his wife and daughters here to live. Pa was delighted to have some family with him at last, here in America. Uncle was invited by Ma to stay with us as long as he had to and told not to worry about a thing.

That is exactly what he did—he stayed and stayed and stayed, getting on everyone's nerves, more each day, with not a mention of his family coming to America. Pa found him several suitable jobs, including our family business, but they were not to his liking. Finally, when he started criticizing the way Pa was running the business and the way Ma was running the house, that became the beginning of the end. He ate, drank, and criticized, and he was gone. One day we woke up and he was no longer there, and we were told that he had to return to Brazil on an emergency.

Allie always said that she could tell something was wrong because Pa was so sad for a long time after that. Much later, when Pa's brother Giuseppe, in Verzino, was told of these happenings, he told Pa that he knew it was going to happen, but he was praying that it wouldn't, because Pasquale did the same thing in Verzino.

It was three years later when we got word that Pasquale was killed by lightening in Brazil. By Pasquale's word only, he left a wife and five daughters. Pa and Giuseppe tried to get in touch with the family for a long time, but to no avail. Did he have a family? We will never know, I think.

BACK TO BEVERLY

Right about now, you might be wondering where we all slept in this small house on West Dane Street. Well, maybe you're not wondering at all about it, but let me tell you anyhow. First, allow me to try to explain our living quarters, and this is possible only after Pa rebuilt the whole house. There was a small room on the southwest corner, facing the backyard—corner closest to Pinciaro—where Mary and Allie got their sleep. Then, into the big room, facing the street, where Bud and Luffy slept on one side of the room and Ned and Americo (*sounds like the national anthem*) on the other side. Now, you go into the hallway, and directly to the right, in another small room that faces the backyard, Joe slept there, alone. Turn left, out of the big room, and then a sharp right and a bigger new room for Jenny and Fanny to sleep in. Of course, Ma and Pa slept on the other side of the stairs, in the new corner room, facing the bakery.

The above living space was only possible because Ma and Pa produced *so* many children (or short employment lists) that he was forced to call in some carpenters to make room for the hordes. So, he removed the top half floor and expanded the second floor, adding two rooms over the yard and supporting them on three columns and a column of bricks on the garage roof. On the front, he closed in the front porch that abutted the sidewalk, went straight up to the second floor, and created a sun parlor running the width of the domain. He installed a new roof and all new clapboard and painted everything a light yellow.

We were a GO! Now, we could all sleep comfortably, two to a bed, except for his highness Joe, the oldest man boy, the assistant baker, the second chair, Mr. Supremo, himself. He slept alone, had his own bed, and yes, he had his own closet for his own beautiful clothes.

... that I used to borrow all the time, without his permission. In fact, my graduation picture shows me in his new, beautiful, camel hair sport coat. When Joe saw that picture, he nearly ... well, you know ...

Our last and final Lauranzano first saw the light of day in Ma and Pa's bedroom, delivered by Dr. Maiuzzo, his first Lauranzano delivery. Her name was given to her by the top three—Phyllis, the only Americanized name in the family. The others born in Beverly, with the exception of Enrico, were delivered by Dr Kidarski.

I could never understand why Ma and Pa never used poor Mariamala again. She sure did a great job with me. It only cost Pa a quarter. Plus, I had a friend for life. Of course, I was born on the 18th day of May and was not registered at City Hall until the 21st day of May. So, when is my birthday?

Phyllis was petted and fondled. She was cute, and everyone said, "She looks just like Ma." But by now, babies born to us at 36 West Dane Street didn't get us too excited. They were just routine in our house, like mixing a batch of dough. We were even taking bets that Ma and Pa were not finished yet.

Now, there were ten—five girls and five boys. Would there be more?

The family business was moving along at a satisfactory pace. After six years in operation, Pa was still picking up new customers. A good example was the development of the Beverly Farms area, where newly immigrated Italians were moving in and building their own homes, where they planned to raise their families. They found employment as groundskeepers with Beverly's very rich citizens, who built their palatial homes on Beverly's beautiful seashore—citizens like Cabot, Sears, Frick, and others.

These newly arrived Italians sought Pa out for their food, on credit, because no one knew them yet or would vouch for them. The Italian immigrants got paid the end of every month, if they had a job, and they had no cash to pay for their food, job or no job. Pa agreed to supply their every need—fresh bread three times a week and all the groceries they required for the month, pasta by the twenty-five-pound box, cheese, tonic, olive oil, to mention a few items. The last day of the month, they got paid, and like clockwork, Pa got paid. Some did not have a job as yet and could not pay Pa, but there were no exceptions. Pa supplied them all. When finally they landed their job, they paid Pa in full. They were even given a cheaper price by Pa than they would have paid in the store. They were very good and dependable people who grew to love Pa like he was one of their own. Families like Spiridigliozzi, DiFazio, Albano, *Rizza, *Fiore, DiPalma, Campagnola, Cerro, Zambello, Nardella, and others.

Ralph Fiore, the youngest son, gave his life on Iwo Jima; and Tony Rizza, during D Day, the invasion of Europe.

The relationship with these fine and generous Italian immigrants went on for many years, and the Lauranzano boys got to know them all well (*particularly the assistant in charge of sales— that's me*). There were several DiFazio families, and I remember the patriarch lived way into the woods where their employer kept a bird sanctuary. The dirt road that led to their house did not get plowed very expeditiously during snow storms, and guess who had to walk the quarter of a mile to deliver their bread, with snow up to his a-a-a-a-ahips? Yup, you guessed correctly, yours truly, the assistant in charge of sales and doing his job. B-r-r-r-r.

Years later, when Joe ran the business, he mentioned many times how the Beverly Farms route was a money loser. But, to his credit, out of respect for Pa's relationship with the people of Beverly Farms, he kept the service going. But of course, even though I was doing other things, he would call me to do it. The Beverly Farms route, oh, the joy of it. I got into my first car accident coming from there, and I didn't even have a license to drive.

Pa had the regular retail routes in Salem, Peabody, and Beverly, as well as the wholesale customers, restaurants, and stores. We served them all. The people of Beverly knew the Columbus Bakery was in Beverly to stay because they loved Pa's nourishing bread. No one ever made Italian bread like Pa did, before or after, and eighty-eight years later, the bakery is still doing business from the same location— one of the oldest business establishments in the City of Beverly.

PA'S BEST FRIEND

Ernesto Zambello lived alone on the corner of Roundy and Mechanic Streets. He was a professional paper hanger and painter and he was Pa's best friend and mentor. When he wasn't working, he was always in the bakery or the pizzeria with Pa.

Mr. Zambello came from Italia alone and had a wife and son still living in Italia. His wife had no desire to join him in America. He didn't mind *that* so much, but he did miss his son. He wrote many letters to his wife imploring her to send their son to him in America, but she always declined. Several years later, she died, and his son finally came to America as an adult. The son stayed a while but then went back to Italia, and Mr. Zambello remained Pa's friend and mentor for the rest of their lives.

Mr. Zambello spoke English fluently and helped Pa and Ma with the language. He even taught Ma to write her name because Ma had no formal schooling, and Mr. Zambello taught Ma quite a bit of English and a lot about living the "Americano" way. He was Pa's "tre sette partener" as well (partner in tre sette, an Italian card game), and a frequent guest on our summer outings at Chebacco Lake or wherever they designated to be the location of our next outing. My sisters did not care for him because they thought he dominated too much of Pa's time. But Pa respected Ernesto's intellect and learned from it. Pa knew people and knew how to get the most out of them. He genuinely liked people.

THE PIANO AND THE PHILCO RADIO

One Saturday, when Pa was working in the bakery, a man came in to ask him if he was interested in purchasing a player piano, inclusive of a bench. Pa asked where it was, and he said that it was sitting outside on his truck. They adjourned the meeting to the outside to view this music maker, and by now, we were all around Pa and the man, wondering what was going on. Pa, obviously, liked what he saw and asked the man what he wanted for the piano. The man asked for twenty-five dollars. Pa offered him five, and the man took the five, unloaded the piano, and put it in place, in the front room of the house. For that, Pa gave him an extra two dollars.

Exploring Pa's new acquisition, we found a whole bunch of music rolls inside the bench, so we sat, played, and sang for hours. This had to be the steal of the century because we sat at that piano, pumped those pedals, and sang for the rest of day, and for years after that.

Allie was always the pedal pusher and led us in many songs, like: "The Very Thought Of You," "You Are My Sunshine," "Melancholy Baby," "When The Moon Comes Over The Mountain," "Ramona," and many others. Her favorite was "Ramona." It was introduced in 1928 in a movie with the same name, sung by Delores Del Rio. We never gathered around that player piano that Allie didn't bring that roll out—several times—for us to sing to. She just loved that tune and the lyrics, *s-o-o-o much*!

For you, Allie, I will now sing "Ramona" to you, like I used to, so many years ago.
Ramona, I hear the mission bells above Ramona, they're ringing out our song of love
I press you, caress you
And bless the day you taught me to care I'll always remember
The rambling rose you had in your hair
Ramona, when the day is done, you'll hear my call
Ramona, we'll meet beside the waterfall I dread the dawn

When I awake to find you gone
Ramona, I need you, my own

Allie, I swear I can hear us singing around that player piano—you, Mary, Jenny, Ned, Fanny, Luffy, and me. (Buddy and Phyllis joined us when they grew up a little.) Sometimes, you'll remember, you were tired from pumping the pedals and I got down on my knees and pumped the pedals with my arms. I remember even Joe's voice among us, and Mary leading the singing. Mary had the best voice, and she let everyone know it by singing out in her beautiful soprano voice. We loved her voice.

Pa didn't stop with a player piano. He brought into our front room a new Philco console radio. When Allie didn't have us singing, we were listening to *The Shadow*; *Mr. District Attorney*; *Frank Merriwell, The All American Boy*; *Inner Sanctum*; *The Lone Ranger*; *The Jack Benny Show*; *Amos and Andy*; the Red Sox games; the fights; and many others. But the most important program of all—that we had to disappear and *get out of Allie's way for,* and pretend we were far, far away for—was *Myrt and Marge.* That was Allie's favorite program, and it came on every Saturday night, and we had better make ourselves scarce, "or death would become a blessing."

A player piano, a Philco radio, a Buick Roadster—no wonder Pa joined the Beverly Republican club, he had it all. But it could have also been to supply the bread for all their banquets, or large flat pizzas for their beer and wine parties. He did supply them, and for the Italian Community Club too, with all the above goodies, but Pa also attended as a guest. That's when Pa, most always, got into trouble.

I was about eight or nine at this time, and when Pa attended those affairs, and wasn't home by the witching hour, Ma would get us out of bed and send us out to fetch him home. Pa was a hard worker, and working 24/7 was quite difficult, so I think he deserved to let loose once in awhile, but Ma thought enough was enough, as she put it, and we had to fetch him and sort of guide him home. When we found him, he never gave us an argument. He just came right along with us, and Ma would put him to bed.

I don't know what was said or done in their bedroom, but the next morning, everything was forgiven and forgotten.

The Italian Republican Club, very popular in those days, was located on Rantoul Street, where the aluminum window place was, next to that little building, where Freddy Appoloni had his barber shop. The club moved to larger quarters during the mid-thirties, to the second floor of Rubinstein's Sheet Metal Shop, across from the

Venetian Cafe. That was a more difficult place to guide Pa home from because of the steep stairway. God, we were always afraid he would fall down those steep stairs.

But like I said, this wasn't a common occurrence. I just tell this story about Pa to show that he was, after all, human.

MARY CAN SING

At one time, about 1937, every Saturday night at the Ware Theater they had amateur night, with prizes, and the Lauranzano kids and our friends attended regularly.

One of our friends, Tony Corte, and our cousin Jerry entered on a regular basis, singing the only song they knew, "South Of The Border." A neighborhood girl, Marie Parisella, also entered on a regular basis and won several times, singing Jeanette McDonald's "Rose Marie." This song just happened to be my sister Mary's best song too, and we thought Mary was better than Marie Parisella. We would go home and beg Mary to enter because we thought she could win, and maybe she would be discovered and become rich and famous.

But she never did, and got herself married instead, and how can you get discovered that way. So, we had to be satisfied with singing around the piano and going to the Ware Theater to get the free dishes for Ma.

While on the subject of movie theaters, I have to recall for you how exciting it was for us to go to the movies on Saturday afternoon when we were wee ones. There were three movie houses in Beverly at that time, from, like, 1932 to 1936. There was the Ware, now the Cabot Cinema; and the Larcom, on Walnut Street; and the Strand, on Cabot Street, in the Union Building or next to it. On Saturday, there was always a long line at the Ware. The front of the Ware was an open foyer, with the box office in the center of the open foyer and still photos, under glass, on all the walls, advertising the coming movies. The doors were on the inside wall of the foyer, where the ticket collector stood. If we were late getting there and the lines were almost to West Dane Street, we would find someone we knew that was close to the box office, like maybe my sister Fanny or a friend, to buy our tickets.

Once inside, it would be bedlam. Shouting, whistling, and any type of noise, as long it was noise. You could not hear yourself talk or think, so we made noise, too.

By the time the movie started, it was standing room only. I mean, every Saturday, standing room only. That's when an usher's job was something very cool.

When the lights dimmed, and the curtains opened, and the lion roared for MGM, or Lady Liberty came on for Columbia, or Paramount's flashlights searched the skies, or Paramount News started with their blaring signature, or Stan Laurel and Oliver Hardy's signature song came on, or the Three Stooges started, a cheer would erupt from all the kids in the audience that you could probably hear in Gloucester. Then, quiet as a mouse! It was remarkable. It was a kid's world—kids only were allowed.

Let them be kids now, for these were the same children that would grow up one day to lay their life on the line for their country. Amen to that.

SUNDAY MORNING

What I remember most about that time in our lives was Sunday morning, particularly in the wintertime. We awoke Sunday morning with the aroma of frying meatballs (*Ma called them "poopats"*) and Ma singing in the kitchen.

One of us would venture down to get the *Sunday Advertiser* from the outside kitchen stoop and pull the comic strips, and bring them to the bedroom, and we would lounge in bed, spending the morning with "Popeye the Sailor", "Dick Tracy," "Terry and Pirates," "Bringing Up Father" ("Maggie and Jiggs"), "Flash Gordon," "Gasoline Alley," "Barney Google," "Snuffy Smith," "The Dragon Lady," "Little Orphan Annie," and "Annie Rooney," just to name a few, after which, Ma treated us to a few fried meatballs before they went into the pasta sauce. Oh, and what a treat that was!

That's why, year after year, every Sunday morning, Allie still carried on with that tradition that Ma started so very long ago. They're never quite as delicious as the meatballs Ma made on those cold Sunday mornings (a close second though), but the memory of them is still good.

THE NIGHT JOE DIDN'T COME HOME

As I previously said, Joe was a problem that Pa could not master. Joe worked hard for Pa and did good work even at a young age. He was a natural baker and was never afraid of hard work, but as far as Pa was concerned, Joe had a serious problem. Joe's problem was that he was an independent thinker who did not always coincide with the way Pa thought. Pa could not abide that condition and often brought this problem to Joe's attention.

But of course, Joe, in his opinion, did not see this as a problem. He often advised Pa of this, but could not convince Pa of this. Joe finally came to the conclusion, all by himself, that it would be best if he parted company with Pa to seek his fortune elsewhere, without Pa's constant interference. So, he and his best buddy, Freddy Valentine, set off for the City Of Detroit to seek their fortune. Why Detroit, you ask? Freddie had relatives there, and they planned that they would live with them, and pay them room and board after they found a job.

Yes, they thought they would. Smack in the middle of the worst depression the world has ever seen.

Pa noticed Joe was among the missing when he did not come home that night. He informed the police and the police started a search, to no avail. For the next day and a half, we fretted and cried, particularly Ma. You have never seen so much wailing and crying— you would have thought Ma was at one of her wakes. Late the next evening, when they were almost two full days away from home, we received a call from the Detroit police, advising of their "capture".

The boys were put on the next bus to Boston. Pa met them there and brought them home. I don't know what happened to Freddie at his home, but I know what happened in our home. It was the first and only time that I ever experienced Pa hitting one of us kids. I remember praying that night that it would never happen again, because Pa took off his belt and gave Joe the beating of his young life, which

Joe never forgot. This took place on the kitchen floor, with all us kids looking on. When it was over, Pa looked at us and said, "Go to bed!" When I think I noticed Pa's eyes filling up, we went off to bed. Ma cried and wailed from the second Joe was declared missing, through the beating and the demand to go to bed. She then picked her fourteen-year-old son up off the floor and put him to bed, both of them in tears.

ALLIE HAS HER WAY

It was 1934, and Pa received a letter from his older brother Giuseppe, in Verzino, informing Pa that his son and Pa's nephew, Giovanni, passed away at the age of 26. Pa hardly knew him because the boy was born in 1908, and Pa left Italy for the last time in 1909. But still **...**

Allie left school that same year when she reached the legal quitting age of sixteen because she found employment with Woolworth's "five and dime" on Cabot and Federal Streets. It was not as though she was a dropout, like you would be in our present culture. The year 1934 was a depression year, and practically everyone at her age quit school to go to work. Not that Allie had to quit school—it was her preference. In fact, Pa tried to stop her from doing so, but no one changed Allie's mind once set. Her first position with the conglomerate chain store was assistant soda jerk.

I remember the argument that ensued when she broke the news to Pa and Ma that she was leaving school. "Why?" they asked. "Because I'm bored," Allie replied. Now, an audience started to gather to witness this historical event. Our parents let it be known, in no uncertain terms, that they were not very happy with this turn of events. Allie ended up locking herself in the bathroom and not coming out until bedtime, and no one said anything to her, except, **"WHEN ARE YOU COMING OUT OF THERE? I HAVE TO GO!"** And Allie shouted back, ***"IT'S TOO BAD, I'M NOT COMING OUT,"*** as she sobbed away.

Often, I have gone back to the bakery, which our nephews Joey and Jimmy now run, and when I go by the bathroom, I always think of Allie when she quit school and made that bathroom her home for a day and her bastion of resistance.

Anyway, that was the start of Allie's memorable career with Woolworth. It didn't take long before she was in charge of the soda fountain. She hired girls that became her lifelong friends, like Margaret Accomando, Thelma Fox and her sister Beth,

Lorraine Tremblay, Gracie Foss, and others. Did this affect her position as second in command of the Lauranzano household? That's an emphatic no, and I ought to know. Allie worked all day at Woolworth, and when she finished there, she came home and helped Ma to get our supper, and got us settled down if some of us didn't have something to do in the bakery after supper. (We used to call it supper all the time; later, it became dinner.)

Mary was still working in the store and was now, more or less, the manager. She also quit school and was working the store fulltime.

Jenny, thank God, graduated from high school. She was in the third-ever graduating class from the new high school on Conant Street and Sohier Road. (It is now Briscoe Middle School). After graduation, in 1933, Pa sent her to the Salem Commercial School to learn accounting, and that is what she was doing for Pa, minding his books and finances. Later, she became a baker and a pizza maker, and she worked very hard for Pa until we grew up enough to help her out.

Joe was still in school at the age of fifteen and anxious to quit. He would get up way early, mix a batch of dough for Pa, and then go to school. Returning at three, he helped Pa deliver the bread until finished. He came home to eat supper, and then went out with his friends, when he should have been going to bed because he got up so early. Running away, however, was a thing of the past and best forgotten.

Ned was twelve and was on-the-job training and trying to be a baseball player. He helped Joe in the bakery before school and after school. For such a young guy, only twelve, he worked almost as hard as Joe, but his heart was just not in it. The baseball diamond was his dream.

I was ten and trying to enjoy life by making it miserable for Allie and Mary. Mary was so cheap with the good stuff in the store,

she squeaked. And Allie whacked me behind the head all the time, mainly because my heels made black marks on her newly-waxed kitchen floor. She always said if I didn't stop ruining her floor, she was going to kill me. All of those whacks behind the head? Maybe that's my problem today.

Fannie was eight and going on thirty. She helped Ma and Allie around the house. Even at eight, she was a constant reader. Put a book in front of her and she devoured it before you could say, "Read this." She also loved to listen to Ma sing arias from different operas. It's really odd that you would hear Ma singing in Italian, sort of to herself, and you didn't realize she was singing an aria from some well known opera. Fannie always knew and tried to sing along with her. That always amazed me.

Young Raphael (Rufaluch is what Ma always called him, and from that name, everyone started calling him Luf or Luffy) was just starting school. Bud and Phyllis were still babies and under Ma's personal care.

MA DID IT ALL

I gave you Ma's schedule, but I did not mention her seasonal chores, like every fall, she procured or was given a few bushels of tomatoes. She would spend a whole weekend preparing and putting them in jars—putting up the tomato preserves. Fannie and I had to put the tops on the jars with the rubber band and be sure they were airtight. Ma always used her own prepared and preserved tomatoes in her pasta sauce, which, of course, was the best sauce in the world.

Home brewed beer was another of her specialties. In the same little pantry, off the kitchen, she made and bottled her own beer. And I can personally assure you that it was delicious. Fannie and I had to put the caps on. At first, it was the bottles with their own rubber gasket, with the wire to tighten the fit. Later, she got the newly invented mandrel-type bottle capper, with metal caps that Fannie and I had to operate. At first, Ma had me fill the bottles with the siphon hose, but I was putting more on the floor than in the bottles, so she fired me and had Allie do it, and I was demoted to the capping operation. *Zounds, what a revolting development that was!*

But, best of all, she preserved rum soaked cherries. **WOW**, they were good! Ma didn't know that Ned and I dipped into them now and then until she started to suspect and counted them, and then she periodically checked the count, and we were caught. She did the cherry preserves mainly for her brothers—they loved them. Ned and I became quite tipsy a couple of times that I can remember. Ma only scolded us, but she made the mistake (*or was it a mistake?*) of telling Allie, and that is all we heard about for the next several days. She told everybody. And yup, you guessed it, more whacks behind my head.

Ma also preserved any fruit that was picked in the area or became plentiful during the picking season, like pears, peaches, and apricots. All her preserves were stored in a small, cemented room in the basement of the house that had served as the coal bin before Pa went modern and installed an oil burner.

Early 1930s, prohibition era, Pa bought maybe one hundred bushels of red and green grapes every year that were always delivered during the fall, on a Saturday night. Joe, Ned, and I carried them through the back yard and through the oversized window into the cellar. Now that I think about it, that must have been the reason for the oversized window. I used to wonder. Pa stayed in the cellar while we handed him bushel after bushel, and he stacked the bushels the way he wanted them.

For the next few days, we ate a lot of grapes, until Pa started the wine making process. The worst job during the whole process was washing out the barrels, which was a very difficult task, at best. This was assigned to Ned and I. When we thought we were finished, we weren't too surprised to learn that we weren't and had to do them again.

Pa made the wine, as did all the Italian guys in the neighborhood—they were all expert at the task. Pa had his own crusher and everything else he needed. That was one thing he kept for himself; he wouldn't let any of us help make the wine. I guess it reminded him so much of his home, of long ago, in Italia.

Pa loved his wine. When all his neighbors finished their own wine, they tasted each other's efforts to see who did the best. When he was working, he always drank a glass with his lunch, but because it was a work day, he always diluted the wine with orangeade. He would eat a big lunch, then put his head down on the table and nap for fifteen or twenty minutes, and when he woke up, he was good to go. No one disturbed him—not that we feared to, but because we knew he needed the rest. Ma taught us that, early on, in no uncertain terms.

The wood pile was an experience not to be forgotten. To light the fire in the baking oven each morning, it was necessary to start the fire with kindling wood, as you would any fire. Well, Pa always supplied his own kindling by buying the wood, all chopped in little pieces, from the Kelleher Ice and Coal Company. They delivered this to Pa with the delivery of the coke that Pa used to bank his fires with.

One warm spring day, I was in the fifth grade at the time, and I was walking home from the Washington School, enjoying life in general. I reached the end of Chase Street, turned the corner and faced our yard, and almost fainted. There in the yard was a pile of wood so high that it reached the second floor of the house. It was a pile of old, used boards that must have come from some old, torn-down building. Pa was standing there with an axe—no, actually, it was two axes, one for me and one for Ned, and Ned wasn't home yet. I have to say it, I almost messed my pants. Pa said that the two of us had to chop all this wood to save the family a ton of money, and I was to start immediately because this pile of rotten wood did not look good in our yard. When Ned got home, he did mess his pants (*just kidding*), but he was upset because he had baseball practice and he couldn't make the practice—while Pa was watching, anyhow.

Here's the best part of the story (*just kidding again, it was really the worst, in two ways*). Ned took his first chop and got a splinter in his eye and had to be rushed to the hospital, and I was stuck with the whole load of wood. The hospital bill was staggering, twice what Pa would have paid Kelleher for the already-chopped wood. But Pa bought the pile of wood every year anyway, and Ned and I had to transform all those huge, used boards into little pieces, every year, until 1938, when Pa put in the oil burner.

Thank God that Pa believed in new technology. No more wood piles.

John Giulebbe finally got fed up with Pa's griping about wanting him to show up on time for work, so he quit the job. It wasn't enough that he quit, but he had to keep telling Pa off and swearing at him in the Italian language all the way up West Dane Street, until he turned the corner at Rantoul Street. Even then, we could still hear him. This is when my brother Joe got to be assistant to the first baker, after Pa took over the first baker/owner job. Now, this arrangement caused some consternation because Pa was also the sales manager, meaning he was the sole deliverer of our bread to our customers.

To solve this problem, Pa hired my idol, John DiRubio, as driver and deliverer for the Columbus Bakery. Now, you have got to know that John DiRubio was the elite athlete of Beverly. He was the high school football and baseball captain in 1929, and became a professional baseball player, first baseman in the Canadian League. I couldn't wait to get out of school and help him on the truck. He used to pick me up after school, and after deliveries, he would take me to the Cooney Field to watch him play first base for the Beverly Macabees, in the Beverly Twilight League. If you know Cooney Field in those days, they had a football grandstand in centerfield, some four hundred feet from home plate. John DiRubio parked at least one every game in those seats.

If they had as many teams in the majors then as they do now, John would have been famous. What a guy!

Unfortunately, John DiRubio did not last long working for the family business. He liked working with our family, but he fell in love and wanted to get married, and he felt he had to earn more money then Pa could pay. So, like everyone else in Beverly, he went to work for the United Shoe and married the very, very beautiful oldest Julius girl, who lived with her family above the Italian Community Center on Rantoul Street. She was so beautiful that everyone was in love with her (*even me*). I heard rumors to the effect that Mary, our sister and store manager, had a crush on John. But that is just an unconfirmed rumor.

To solve this problem, Pa persuaded John Giulebbe to return to work, with Joe as his boss rather than Pa. Pa thought that would work out better for John, and Pa would return to the truck. Of course, Joe was all for this because it allowed him to leave school and work steady in the bakery as the boss. Joe became a very good baker, much better than John, actually, but Ma kept an eye on Joe and saw that Joe kept his respect for his Uncle John.

Ma would say to Joe, "No monkey business, Giusepp, or else," and Joe never "dissed" our Mother or Uncle John, you have got to give him that.

But Ma was disappointed soon after, when John quit again because he could not stand Joe telling him what to do—again, swearing all the way up the street and around the corner. I think, after that, even Ma gave up on him. Then, poor Jenny had to assume John's duties in the bakery and, then at night, with Pa, making pizza. Jenny worked very hard for the family business until Ned was old enough to assume the duties in the bakery.

Pa continued the practice of picking me up after school to help on the truck. I didn't mind because I enjoyed doing my part, except chopping wood, but I knew, even then, that I was not going to quit school for the family business. Not that I was that fond of school. I just didn't like working the family business all that much. You have to keep in mind that the big depression caused most kids to quit school in those days and get a job, or else go into the Civilian Conservation Corp (called the CCCs). Several of the neighborhood kids went into the CCCs, and I never heard anyone mention "dropout."

MARY WEDS

In 1936, Mary announced that she would wed Angelo Pinciaro, our next door neighbor and the iceman for Kelleher Ice and Coal. He delivered the ice to our store and house, and evidently, to everyone's surprise, he got to know our Mary quite well. At first, Pa—like any Italian man thinks he has to do—he objected to the marriage. After being educated to the facts, he relented and welcomed Angelo into the family.

Ma and Pa planned a big wedding. Mary chose a wedding dress and planned to be very beautiful at her wedding. Pa hired the Pythean Castle on Federal Street for the reception. He hired a band and made a million sandwiches and had a million cases of soda delivered by the American Seltzer Company and many jugs of the "homemade stuff." He ordered a wedding cake from Irving Pastries on Cabot Street, and we were a go, with one exception.

In our many travels together, delivering bread and all, Pa promised me a new suit for the wedding, with a vest and long pants. It was going to be purchased from the haberdasher who went from house to house to sell his wares. He measured me and promised delivery of a charcoal grey suit by the end of the following week, plenty of time for the wedding. When my beloved suit came, unfortunately for me, Pa had to cancel because of his lack of funds, and I ended up with just a new pair of long pants and a new polo shirt. The disappointment was so great, I used to go behind the garage and cry every day for a week (but this time with no vanilla ice cream). Allie utilized the bathroom, and I used the back of the garage. Both served their purpose.

I did enjoy the wedding, however. We danced and slid all over the slippery dance floor, and it was the first time we saw our mother dance the Tarantella. It seemed like every Italian/American in the city was present at the reception. All the sandwiches were eaten and all the soda and wine were drunk. The dancing went on and on to the melodious tunes of The Black and White Orchestra. I think I even saw Pa dance one or two with Ma and Mary. *Oh what fun it was that day*!

Mary tied the knot, moved out of the house, and rented an apartment on Whitney Ave with Angelo, and with all new appliances and furniture, fresh out of Kransburgs. Pa closed down the store, applied for a beer license, and got it. The store became a pizzeria.

It was named The Columbus Pizzeria, and a new era began in the lives of the Lauranzano family.

It was 1936, my first year at Briscoe Junior High School, near Ellis Square. I was delivering bread with Pa every morning before school until Ma interceded and made me stop the bread thing and go right to school. Ned was mixing dough every morning before school. Well, maybe not every morning. Joe was working with Jenny and getting along pretty good. Pa was delivering the bread and concentrating on his new and exciting pizza business, but building a very good route nonetheless.

First, Pa had to redo the present facility to accommodate the beer and wine license. He tore down the petition that accommodated the store and took more of the bakery with the new pizzeria petition, lengthwise. He took the whole of the building with the exception of about fourteen feet, for the width of the bar, short of the yard wall, for a foreshortened store. Lengthwise, for the store, he petitioned just past the cellar door. He moved the icebox into the small store area, built a counter, added paper and string, and we were go to sell our bread from there. Add the slicing machine and cold cuts for the icebox, and we were go to sell sliced cold cuts with our bread. He built a cake and

sliced bread stand against the outside wall, and we were go to sell sweets with our cold cuts and bread.

On the bar side, he built a bar running from the street wall to the bakery side, just short of a door he put in to enter the bakery. A big mirror hung on the wall on the back of the bar, with jugs of commercial wine along the bottom of the mirror. He put a Coca Cola cooler on the street end, behind the bar, holding soda and ice, and built his own booths, all along the walls. And lastly, he had the beer taps, with coils and all, installed, and he brought in the kegs of Houlahan's, Narragansett, Ballantine, and other beers. He covered the coils with ice, got everyone ready to help with the work, put Jenny in charge of pizzas, and he was ready for opening night. The man was amazing.

As it turned out, so was Jenny.

OUR UNCLES RALPH AND GUIDO

You might think that we have forgotten Ma's brothers in Fall River and Newport, but there is no chance of that ever happening. They visited their sister, with their entire brood, at least six times a year, and we visited there, maybe, twice a year. I do not know why, but it always seemed like they had more opportunity for visits then Pa did. When there was a visit, either way, we always had to hit the mattresses on the floor. We would get after Pa to go for a visit as much as possible, but he never would close the family business for any visit. I think it just didn't interest him. Anyway, Raphael is now known as Uncle Ralph and Guido as Uncle Guido, and out of respect, this is how they'll be referred to from here on in.

When Uncles Ralph and Guido came to Beverly for one of their infrequent visits, the first thing they did was give each of us kids a dollar, and the party would start. Ma cooked a dinner of a million courses, and unless you experienced one of her specially prepared dinners, you can not possibly imagine how delicious the whole dinner was. Following dinner, all kinds of fruit and nuts and Ma's baked Italian pastries were served up. After which, the table was cleared and we got our pennies out, which we had been saving for this very night, and then we dealt the cards for a mean game of sette mezza (seven and a half). We played until the wee hours—Ma, Pa, Uncles, the girls, and some of us kids, but me for sure. *Oh, what fun we used to have. To this day, we are a family of card players.*

Sometimes, I thought that our Uncles came to Beverly just to show off their new cars. It seemed like every time they came, they had the latest model Oldsmobile. The first automatic shift I ever witnessed was on Uncle Ralph's brand new 1939 Oldsmobile. But in those days, Ma was her happiest when she was with her brothers. Absence makes the heart fonder, right? Whatever it was, we got great benefit from it, *whatever it was.* When our uncles visited, Ma made it seem like Thanksgiving and Christmas, all rolled into one. However, we did sincerely love our uncles, we really, really did. We looked forward to their visits with great anticipation, and we were very blue whenever they left.

LOOKS LIKE PA SHOULD HAVE STAYED IN NEWPORT
JUST KIDDING

At this time, 1937, Uncle Guido was doing so well with the bakery that he built a new home in Middleton, RI (on Rte. 114). Actually, he put up what was then considered a mansion. He had yellow bricks imported from Italy and red tile for the roof, again imported from Italy, on a large lot of land, maybe three acres. He also had three bungalows built on the land, each with kitchen, living room, and one bedroom, that he rented to naval officers who were attending the War College and their wives. Also, there was a two car garage, made from the same yellow bricks and red tile. The house had a long driveway, a spacious lawn with landscaping, and a small balcony on the front of the house. It was a one-floor dwelling, with a large Italian kitchen, a large dining room, large living room, three bedrooms, and two full baths.

Looks like Pa should have stayed in Newport—just kidding, you couldn't get Pa out of Beverly with a canon.

Uncle Guido had Victor and Hecter in training to take over the bakery. Hecter was Ned's age and Victor was Joe's age. On visits to or fro, they use to hang out. But in 1937, Joe wasn't around much—he was out of school, grown up, and kept his own council, and so did Victor. However, Victor was still in school, and he eventually graduated from Newport's Roger Williams High School, from where, eventually, all of Uncle Guido's children graduated. You have to give that to Uncle Guido, or it looks more like Aunt Teresa's influence.

Of course, we visit that house to this day because Victor and his wife, the very gracious and lovely Monica, now own the property. Monica is a lifelong resident of Newport, and she and Victor have been married for a thousand years. They have made it known thousands of times that we are always welcome there, and urge us to visit, but as is the case in many families in today's society, we just do not visit enough. It's hard to believe, but our parents visited each other more often than we do ...

... and they didn't have routes 128 and 24 and high speed cars.

Uncle Ralph, I think, visited us more than Uncle Guido. Uncle Ralph was more sociable and, I think, got along with Pa a little better. One visit in the early thirties, he visited us in Beverly, accompanied by his father and mother, as he always was, since they lived with him. They were very old and cranky, or so the Lauranzano kids thought, anyhow. But this time, unbeknown to Ma and Pa, Uncle brought along their luggage and, unannounced, he said their Mama and Papa wanted to stay in Beverly awhile to visit with their two daughters. Well, Ma was all for that, but Pa was not. They stayed with us in Beverly because Ma said. They took Gennina and Fanny's room, and the girls had to move into the sun parlor. Sleeping in the sun parlor made it seem like you were sleeping on the sidewalk. The girls were not happy campers.

For several months, Grandma gave Ma all the advice she could use for a thousand years. Grandpa sat in the front porch smoking a pipe all day. In all the time they were with us, Santina probably visited her parents twice. And then, it happened—the unforgivable. Allie said something to Grandma that she did not care for that resulted in Grandma pinching Allie, Ma's very own pet, *one very vicious pinch,* and that was the beginning of the end of Grandma and Grandpa's visit to Beverly. Our grandparents' next stay, soon after the pinch heard round the world that caused Allie to be black and blue for months, was Newport and Uncle Guido's new home in Middletown, RI on Route 114.

BEVERLY, MASSACHUSETTS

In 1938, Ned went to high school and I was in the ninth grade at Briscoe. Ned played football for Briscoe the year before, which had a good team because Buzz Foley coached the team. Our bud, Cheecho Filtranti, also played with Ned at Briscoe and high school. We also played for our sandlot team, called the Beverly Night Hawks. We adopted that name because we always practiced at night, on the Beverly Common. We had an excellent team and we were undefeated. We had uniforms donated to us by Guido Scotti, who once sponsored a professional team. He donated the uniforms to the Night Hawks through his younger brother, Billy.

Ned and Cheecho did well with the Night Hawks. They were our star running backs, along with fleet-footed Matt D'allesandro. Although they did well with the Hawks, they did not do well with the high school team. Cheech made a letter and Ned did not because he quit school and joined the army in 1938. If Ned had stuck it out, I'm sure he would have made the football team and the baseball team. He was a good athlete. But, of course, as far as making good in any sport, the Lauranzano boys had one very big obstacle, and that was our Pa.

Coming from his very limited social background, Pa did not believe that athletics was a worthwhile endeavor and tried to discourage us. It was very difficult, but we tried anyway. I remember the summer of 1938, when Ned and I were playing baseball for The Cove Athletic Club, playing twice a week in the Beverly Twi-light League, and we dressed in the garage. We went in one afternoon to dress, and we found the uniforms had been destroyed by Pa. His reasoning was that the game was causing us to neglect our responsibilities with the family business. I guess he was right in a way, but we didn't see it that way at the time. It didn't affect me as much as it did Ned. He was a better baseball player than I was and could have been a lot better with some encouragement from the right places.

Pa tried to stop me from playing football but he didn't get far on that score. No one could have stopped me playing football. When Pa was tending bar in the pizzeria, his customers would show him newspaper articles where I would be mentioned or my picture would be featured, and I guess he sort of got a feeling of pride that altered his feelings about me and football. My efforts in football turned him around enough so that he gave our team a pizza party that even Coach Morris and Mayor McLain attended. Larry McLain, the Mayor's son, was on the team. When Pa saw the Mayor come in the place, Pa was surprised, delighted, and proud.

My friends, I'll tell you the truth. Columbus Pizzeria was jamming that night. The whole neighborhood, or maybe the city, turned out there to see the kids that defeated Beverly's Thanksgiving Day rivals for the first time in eighteen years.

NED'S JAMBOREE

I **know you have to be wondering** what this is all about. NED'S JAMBOREE? I have to dedicate this story to Pa's favorite daughter, later known as Sister Frances, but for now, just plan Fannie. She was number seven in the family, and that's a lucky number. In 1937 and '38, when Pa got rid of his Buick Roadster, we had the left side of our two-car, heated garage empty. Not wanting to see this nice space go to waste, we decided to start a dance club. That was the popular thing to do since the swing bands were so popular and the lindy hop was the rage. We cleaned the garage up, moved the victrola and the long playing records in, and started dancing.

Muzzy Carnevale and his sister Josephine, Bobby Tate, Billy Scotti, Fannie, and others joined us now and again. We started dancing up a storm. Fannie loved it; she couldn't get enough of it. There was Glen Miller, Bennie Goodman, Tommy Dorsey, Jimmie Dorsey, and Fannie's favorite, Harry James, as well as many others. I have to say, we had good, clean fun; even Pa enjoyed watching us dance. We all became darn good dancers, too, in the bargain, and it didn't even take us from our responsibilities, as Pa would say.

I am sure that my sister Fannie fondly remembers NED'S JAMBOREE. We sure cut a rug, eh, Fran?

Up until this point, Ned was an important cog in the bakery, working with Joe and Jenny. He mixed the dough in the morning before school, and joined them again after school and did whatever he could. Pa was working the truck with me as his helper, when he could catch up to me. I was a lineman in football, but to Pa, I was an illusive running back. He could never catch up to me. On a couple of occasions, he even chased me down the street. He never could understand that my schedule was very crowded, and that it came first, with the bakery and truck a very distant second. No siree, Bub, he could not, or rather, he would not understand.

Parents just do not understand what a kid has to do. But seriously, if I wanted to eat, Pa caught up with me most of the time, and I had to work my way to stardom on the truck.

The truck was usually a Chevrolet Panel Truck. Sometimes, the bakery's name was printed on the side panel, and sometimes not, depending on how much "moola" Pa had at the time. One afternoon after school, in 1938, accompanied by my brother Ned, I was driving the truck without a license, doing the Beverly Farms route. We were on our way home via the back way when a car coming the opposite way on Hull Street, somehow, made me nervous. I went too far on the shoulder, hit a large bolder, bounced back on the road, and hit the car that was coming from the opposite direction. The truck had to be towed. Ned had a license and said he was driving, and I was home free but quite shaken up. That was my first accident, but unfortunately, not my last.

Another incident with the bread truck, about that time in our lives, was the adventurous trip to Vermont with two of the McGillivray sisters of Gloucester, Helen and Georgine, along for the ride. These girls were the younger sisters of Betty, who Joe was seeing on a steady basis. Freddy Valentine—one of Joe's best buddies and a friend of the family—and our first cousin Jerry Giulebbe had joined the Civilian Conservation Corp, commonly known as the CCC. They were assigned to a camp in Vermont, near Burlington, and Ned and I got this notion to visit them. We invited the two sisters to join us, and they agreed.

We snuck the bread truck out of the garage by pushing it out of the yard. We coasted it down Chase Street, starting the truck on the clutch, and we were off to Vermont without any idea how far it was. We had a mattress in the back, had a lot of laughs, and a great time was had by all. We reached our destination without trouble, had a nice visit with the guys, and headed home. On the way home, on a lonely road late at night, we blew a tire and had no spare or money, or even if we had money, nothing was open where we could seek aid. We went to a farmhouse for a phone, called Pa to tell him where the truck and his kids were located, and asked him if he could see his way clear to help us get home. We slept in the truck, and about three in the morning, Pa, Angelo, and Joe showed up with the tire and wheel that someone had forgot to put in the truck in the first place, and we drove home.

To this day, I am waiting for the other shoe to fall. Pa never said anything about it, from day one. Surprisingly, he didn't show the slightest bit of anger. When we got home, Ma fed us. Then, Pa told Ned to get in the bakery to help Joe, and told me to get back in the truck to help him deliver bread, and nothing more was said. I might add here, Joe drove the girls home, and I know they were punished. (Or was it punishment? Their punishment was to "never see those two imbeciles from Beverly again," and they didn't.)

Years upon years later, I ran into the McGillivray sisters again at a wedding or a wake, and they still remembered that infamous weekend, when they had "s-o-o-o much fun!."

SPEAKING OF HAVING FUN

Well, Pa kept us busy when we were working in the family business, but when we weren't busy, we tried to have as much fun as possible. In those years, 1936 to 1940, we were pretty independent with our social activities. For instance, I hung out on the corner of Chase and West Dane with neighborhood friends, in front of the variety store run by our friend Florence Starr. There were friends like Freddie Pasquarelli, Frank Filtranti, Bobby Tate, Matt D'allesandro, Guy Allaruzzo, Charley Sharpe, Leo DeSantis, Billy Scotti, and Louie Vitale.

On Sundays, we always dressed our best and, usually, went to the movies at the Ware Theater. Other times, we sat on the steps of the house on the corner and just hung out. Ned hung out with us for awhile, but he went into the Army in 1939. Other times, we played a lot of touch football and baseball, went to dances, tried to make out, you know, good stuff like that. When hanging around on the steps, we bought soda and cake from Florence and we had fun teasing her—a lot, especially about her boyfriends.

I remember the day Freddie Pasquarelli, after graduating high school, went down to Duke University to try out for their football team. Freddie was a left-handed passing tailback, with the single wing. We gave him a big farewell party and he went off by train, and two weeks later, he was back again, a little banged up, but a lot wiser. Sammy Baugh, he wasn't.

Fannie hung out with the girls in the neighborhood, and they were always going to the movies in Salem or Boston. In Boston, they went to see and hear the big bands at the RKO Theater on Washington Street. She loved the big bands, as I did. Ma use to give her an allowance, and she spent it wisely. She saw Glenn Miller, The Dorsey bands, Gene Krupa, Louie Prima, and many others.

When we were younger, like in 1936, for instance, we went to the playground a lot. I played on the baseball team and took part in all the games and crafts. Della Mellei was the instructor. She later married Harry Ball and was the mother of Harry

Ball Jr., a Boston College football star. The Fourth of July, in 1936, I got the thrill of my life when *they took us to a baseball game at Fenway Park*! It was my first time there, and Lefty Grove was the starting pitcher; and I had a conversation with ol' Lefty while he was warming up. That was really having fun and really an experience I never forgot. It was one of the best experiences of my life. Imagine the great Lefty Grove, Hall of Fame pitcher, actually acknowledged me as he walked to the mound at Fenway Park.

Pa always regarded July Fourth as a special day. He thought that this day should be a family day and the family should and would spend it together. So, he planned picnics for that day. Mostly we ended up at Chebacco Lake in Wenham. It was a nice place for family picnics. A couple of times, we went into some woods in some mysterious place that I could never identify. Ma made great eats and we truly had fun on all those family outings. Sometimes, another family would join us. I remember the next-door Pinciaro family once; and another time, Jimmy Nardella and his family; and Uncles Ralph and Guido and families.

During the Fourth of July week, there was always the Sam Sam. This was a carnival sponsored by the United Shoe for the citizens of Beverly. It was held in an empty field on Cabot Street, past Gloucester Crossing, where the Kelly Dealership is now. It wasn't where the playground is because that was wasteland at that time.

We went there everyday when the Sam Sam was there. We used to run all over the place. We watched the older girls kissing and stuff at night with their boyfriends. I told my cousin Lena, years later, how I used to watch her and her boyfriend, who later became her husband Joe DiPalma, smooching at the Sam Sam. She laughed and laughed. The Sam Sam was probably Beverly's greatest and best citywide function ever. It really brought the people of Beverly together, making a tight community. The Sam Sam fireworks display, on the last day, was always exciting. Since that time, I have seen many fireworks displays, but I remember the Sam Sam display most of all.

Other times, Pa saw fit to have his own fun, without his pesky kids around. Many Sundays, he would go to the Italian Community Club and get himself involved with the Bocce court they had in the backyard of the three-story house they occupied. We used to go there and watch him and his cronies play. Four on a side, and playing four on each end, and it was as cutthroat as you could get and still remain friends. Pa started with a fresh DiNapoli stogie between his lips, and when he finished a game, you could hardly see it, it was so tiny. I never could figure out whether he smoked it or ate it. He played all the time, never sitting, because he was always on the winning side. But between games, it was always the boss and second boss, finger game, for the beer, that was really, really cutthroat.

Then, after the bocce games, or when it got dark, whichever came first, they adjourned to the interior of the club to play a favorite Italian card game called tre sette (three seven). This was another of Pa's favorite pastimes that he enjoyed his whole life. Just like after each bocce game, or after each game of tre sette, they played the boss and second boss finger game for the beer. However, we weren't still there watching him. When they went inside, we had to go home, but we were quite familiar with the procedures. We also knew we would be coming back later, to "fetch" him. We were ready.

Let me explain boss and second boss. There was usually a group of six to eight men, depending on how many were involved with the game (or they included anyone else that wanted to join the game by donating a beer). They stood in a circle and threw any amount of fingers they wanted to when someone yelled go. Someone then would add up the amount of fingers thrown and start counting out that number from a pre-determined starting point. The count ends on the gent with the number of the total that the fingers added up to. That gent becomes the first boss of all the beer that all the players paid for or donated. The gentleman following the first boss becomes the second boss of the beer. Now, the first boss has the total amount of beers in front of him that are all his to drink. If he can't drink them all, or prefers not to, the beer that he can't drink, or prefers not to drink, has to go to the second boss, who can drink the rest of the beers himself or, if he prefers, can distribute any amount of the beers to whomever he pleases, The first can't give out any beer, he has to drink or it goes to the second boss. Sometimes, first and second made deals before second got any of the beer. If the second wouldn't deal, sometimes the first drank it all, especially if he didn't want beer to go a certain direction. Therefore, some gents didn't drink at all, they called it going dry, and I mean all night, and some gents got plastered, and I mean plastered.

Many enemies were made in those days because of the first and second boss fingers game. As a matter of fact, if you go by St. Mary's Cemetery on Brimbal Avenue late at night, you can still hear the yelling.

One of our favorite locations for a summer outing, besides Chebacco Lake, was the Dane Street Beach. We always settled between the two large rocks, on the sand at the bottom of the grassy hill. Many of the families in our neighborhood would also have their outing at the beach at the same time. Ma wore her bathing suit that covered all the way to her ankles. She would go into the water with the other women, holding hands and forming a circle; they would then bob up and down, up and down. It was like watching her do the Tarantella. Fondi, where Ma came from in Italia, is located near beaches, so Ma pretty much knew what to do on a beach.

Not so with Pa—he was a mountain man—but he liked being with us on the beach. He even wore a bathing suit and just liked lying around, smoking his stogies, eating Ma's food, and drinking a little of his homemade wine. He did enjoy watching Ma bobbing up and down with her girlfriends. The Lauranzano kids enjoyed eating the food Ma brought, ducking our heads in the water, and rolling down the grassy hill. Of course, it was a bonus for us if we could weasel some money from Ma or Pa to go across the street to the food pavilion for the many goodies they sold there.

Other times, we often walked to the beach on our own. The walk was a good one going *to* the beach, but coming *home*, our lips were always blue and we were always so very hungry after a day in the water that it made the walk home very uncomfortable.

At that time, the Dane Street Beach was one of the best on the East Coast. There was a large beach house in the center of a spacious lawn, with a large, round porch at the entrance and a large, straight porch along the beach, where they kept chaise lounge chairs to use while enjoying the swimmers and the scenery. Inside there were men's and women's dressing rooms, with wall lockers and walk-in lockers, with keys; and shower rooms. Outside were well kept lawns with immaculate paths and beautiful, full-foliage oak trees, which people just loved sitting under and enjoying family picnics. A large bandstand sat regally in the center of the spacious lawn, where we enjoyed band concerts every Sunday with Beverly's own Mr. Lotito as the conductor.

This is just one of the beautiful characteristics about Beverly that Pa enjoyed so much.

THE COLUMBUS PIZZERIA

The pizzeria was going great guns. It caught on like you wouldn't believe. The first couple of weeks, you couldn't get a booth, it was so busy. There were actual lines waiting to get their order in. We were all working, making pizzas and waiting on customers. We couldn't believe it, nor could we handle such a rush. We tried, but service got too slow and the business went down to normal, but still good, after a couple of weeks. Our main competition was John Giulianni's on Rantoul Street, which was a full-menu restaurant. They were doing, like, four hundred pies per day. I guess we were doing about half of that, maybe a little less than half.

The pizzeria took up about half the bakery's square footage, inclusive of the little store/deli we ran. For a little thing, the store did well with bread sold over the counter, cold cuts, milk, sliced bread, imported provolone, a few canned goods, and more. The pizzeria kept Pa busier then he ever thought he would be. He hired a guy to manage the place, but within two weeks, the guy ran off with two weeks worth of receipts. We never saw that guy again. He gave the responsibility to Jenny, who worked her fanny off, making pizzas and managing. It really was too much for her to handle. But she tried very, very hard. Sometimes I think Pa took advantage of her willingness to work so hard, but what do I know?

Pa tended bar and served the booths. The customers came in and ordered at the bar, and Pa served their beer or wine and then brought their pizza to the booth when it was ready. It doesn't appear as though we were organized well, but when Pa or whoever brought you that pizza that you waited twenty-five minutes for, it was one hell of a mouth-watering pizza. No one has ever made as good a pizza since that time.

After the war, Pa bought Corte's building on the corner of Creek and Rantoul Streets, and moved the pizzeria there, with a full liquor license and food other than just pizza. Ma was preparing the food and making the pizzas. It was a Mom and Pop business. But that's another story, for a different time.

For years after, Joanna still made pizza for us every Sunday afternoon, right up to the age of ninety-two, right after Allie's Sunday morning meatballs. We just could not let it go. Ma and Pa left us so much to remember. Their legacy to us was family and tradition, and I guess we never forgot.

The Columbus Pizzeria opened for business in 1937 and sold out in the early 1950s, and to this day, you can still find people that will tell you they have never had a pizza to equal what they once experienced at the Columbus Pizzeria. John Giulianni sold more pizza, but we were always the best.

PA IS INTO SPORTS

One of our earliest interests in sports was not in the national pastimes, like baseball or football, but was one that Pa got us interested in when the "Ambling Alp," Primo Carnera, direct from the land of Pa's birth, was beating all comers in 1930. I know this is hard to believe, but when all the Italian/Americans all over the country were following the exploits of boxer Primo Carnera, Pa was one of them. All the Carnera fights that were aired he listened to intensely, and so did we.

When the first Jack Sharkey/Primo Carnera fight was aired, in 1931, Pa had his ear glued to the radio, and when Carnera lost that fight to Sharkey on points, Pa declared that Carnera was robbed. Pa was really getting "juiced." The second Sharkey fight he could hardly wait for, but when it finally came around in 1933 for the world's heavyweight championship, and Primo won by a knockout in the sixth round, you would have thought that the world suddenly turned to gold. Never mind that every non-Italian/American in the world thought it was fixed, especially in Boston, where all the Irish/Americans and Sharkey lived. "They're just a bunch of poor losers," our Pa declared, and he gloated like you would not believe, and we, his kids, watched and learned while his new hero, Primo Carnera, was crowned the new heavyweight champion of the world.

So, my dears friends, 1935 rolled around and Primo Carnera signed to fight a Jewish kid by the name of Max Baer. "Now," our father exclaimed to anyone that would listen, and that was many, "it is well known that Jewish boys cannot fight well, and he will be trounced by our champion, Primo Carnera." And at this point in time, his kids, watching him with interest, were nodding their heads in agreement, for if anyone knew, it had to be Pa. Well, fight time came around, and the results of the fight became old news, and as history will tell you, the Jewish boy "that could not fight well" gave Primo the worst beating in the annals of boxing. Max Baer knocked poor Carnera down seven times in one round, eleven times in all, and Carnera was knocked out in the eleventh round. Maxie could have ended it sooner, but for some reason, only known to Max Baer, he wanted to punish our hero. *(Max must have heard what Pa said about him.)*

It occurred suddenly, after that fight, that Pa took a disliking to anything pugilistic and did not think boxing existed anymore. However, the children of his loin continued their interest in sports, which Pa had instilled in them early in their lives and always denied that he did. Late in 1935, when Carnera signed to fight the up-and-coming Joe Louis, we tried to persuade Pa to listen to the fight with us, but he had other things to do, and could not and would not be bothered. As everyone knows, Carnera never landed a punch on Joe Louis and was KO'D by Joe Louis in the sixth round ... and that was the end of Primo Carnera, our hero from Sequals, Italy, and of Pa's career as a sports enthusiast and analyst.

PA IS INTO POLITICS

As an entrepreneur, Pa worked very hard making everything work for him and his family. In his spare time, he read quite a lot about American politics in his weekly Italian Progresso newspaper, and he always said to anyone that would listen how different it was from the politics of his native Italia.

It was the year 1936, and a new face was entering the political arena in Massachusetts. A new face, but not a new name, because Henry Cabot Lodge was a senator and was well known in the Massachusetts political arena. His son, however, Henry Cabot Lodge Jr. was not as well known, and he was making a run to fill his father's seat in the United States Senate.

This was all well and good, but what could all this possibly have to do with Pa? Well, I'm getting to that. Just hold on.

It was a hot, summer Saturday night, and Pa was playing a game of tre sette with some of his cronies in the bakery, when a tall, good looking, well dressed gentleman walked into the bakery and introduced himself—yes, you guessed right, it was Henry Cabot Lodge Jr. After the introductions and some conversation, he asked if Pa would help him garner votes in this neighborhood and with his customers. They chatted for hours, and Ma came in with food, some of her fried, homemade sweet Italian sausage sandwiches, cold drinks, and some homemade wine, and they all became well acquainted. When the Lauranzano kids came home from here and there, we all joined them, and our Mr. Lodge became a family friend, whether he thought he was or not.

Pa did campaign for him, and Henry Cabot Lodge Jr. won the election and won Beverly by a great majority, and Pa always thought it was because of him. Who knows, maybe it was. He did get a letter from Senator Lodge thanking him for his hospitality and help. He showed that letter so much that it wore out.

After that campaign for Henry Cabot Lodge Jr., Pa stayed a Republican, but voted for Franklin Delano Roosevelt, as did everyone else in Beverly. His only other active role in politics after Henry Cabot Lodge Jr. was for Daniel E. McLain, the mayor of Beverly. They were good friends, and he always helped the mayor as much as he could.

JOE GETS INTO TROUBLE

Joe, our erstwhile oldest male member of our family, was starting to feel his oats, with his endless wardrobe, starched collared shirts by Sam Lee the Chinese laundryman, new automobile, and being all of nineteen years old, He and his friends Freddy Valentine, our cousin Jerry, and Rocky Papa journeyed to Gloucester every weekend in search of "Gloucester skirt." I have to say that, because of Joe's heavy work schedule in the bakery, he was more mature than his actual age would indicate. At least, that was what he had us all believe.

When our Newport Marcucci cousins Victor and Hector visited, Joe would take them with him and his friends to Gloucester and give them a time they would long remember. They thought Joe was the man of the town, and so did all his friends, and he had many. He was something.

I was hanging in the yard with all the other Lauranzano kids one Sunday afternoon, right after one of Ma's special Sunday meals of rigatoni with rigotta cheese, chicken in sauce, pork in sauce, sausages, and many other delicious items, when we heard a scream from our mother emanating from the kitchen, never heard by any of us before or since. Of course, we all ran into the kitchen, expecting to see our dear mother lying on the floor, dead. But what we saw was my mother about to clout Joe into a thousand pieces and Allie holding her back, while our father was standing there, speechless.

When everyone and everything settled down, we found out, by listening intently with our mouths agape, that Joe had confessed to our parents that he had his Gloucester girlfriend, Betty McGillivray, in a family way. *Yikes, what did this mean? We had no idea. Should we scream, too?*

He further confessed that he had eloped to New Hampshire and tied the knot, so to speak. In those days, New Hampshire had much looser laws governing quick marriages, and Joe and his new bride took advantage. They were now man and wife, with nowhere to live, and would Ma and Pa mind terribly if they lived with us, here in Beverly? And of course, the answer was that they would have it no other way, but Ma seemed like she still wanted to clout Joe into a thousand pieces. We were sure that she would have if Allie wasn't there, proving once again the influence Allie had with our mother.

Betty was Joe's bride, and she moved into Joe's small room, and Joe lost his private room and his closet, and accentually his independence, but he continued working in the bakery with Jenny and Ned and doing well. Betty helped Ma in the house and even helped a little with the family business, but we noticed, with consternation, that she was growing bigger and bigger.

All the time she worked with Ma in the house, I don't believe they spoke one word to each other that either one understood. They got pretty good at sign language though. Of course, when Allie came home, everything was fine again, because she served well as the translator. While all this was going on, the Lauranzano kids never got used to Betty—we just couldn't understand what was going on. We knew she was having a baby, though, and we were looking forward to the blessed event and always wondering when it would happen.

Nine months? What's going to happen in nine months?

FREDDY VALENTINE AND BROWNIE

Freddy was Joe's best friend, and later was to be the witness and best man at Joe's wedding. Fred always walked to our house from his house in Ryalside every day during summer. It's quite a walk, especially walking home—it's uphill all the way. He did this not only because he was Joe's best friend but because he thought of our family as his family. He and Joe went to Gloucester practically every weekend, and when they weren't in Gloucester, they hung out at The Rendezvous, a dive on Park Street, across from the depot, a real "honky tonk." My friends and I used to look through the windows and watch Joe and Freddie and Joe's other friends, like Mooky and Rocky Papa and Jerry, our cousin, socializing and dancing with all those "ladies of the night." We couldn't wait to be a little older so that we could have fun, too. These older guys had all the fun.

One day, on a lazy Sunday summer afternoon, Freddie came waltzing into the yard with this large brown German Shepard dog that had followed him all the way from Ryalside. He was a beautiful dog that immediately took to all of us. It was love at first sight. He ran from one of us to another as though he loved us all equally. Even Ma and Pa welcomed him. We all knew he was a Lauranzano, a natural. That very night, he slept in the house, behind the stove, where he slept every night for the next fifteen or so years, and we named him Brownie ... *and he became a Lauranzano.*

Sister Frances recalls a time when we had been on a family outing and were all tired and driving home. When we reached home, we saw that Brownie had a man cornered in our yard and wouldn't let the man go. When we got there, we got Brownie in control and found that the man was Pa's cousin from Mansfield. Pa apologized profusely, but the man said he was trying the door to see if anyone was home and Brownie interceded. He said Brownie was a good watch dog—he didn't attempt to hurt the man, just control him. He and Pa had a good visit, and Brownie ended up licking the hand of the man from Mansfield. *Good dog!*

We can recall many times when Brownie prevented the little ones from wandering into the street. It might be the reason we did not have any more broken legs from runaway automobiles.

Thanks again, Fred, we were always most grateful to you for bringing Brownie into our lives. We loved him dearly.

OUR BREAD ROUTE

In those early years in the Italian bread business, I think Italian bread was meant to be sold over the counter, at the bakery, so that it could be properly wrapped, *or* so *I say now*. In those days, selling bread from the truck, the bread was unwrapped and was kept in the wooden boxes that you had put the bread in when it was removed from the oven. All we did was stand the bread up in the box so we could place more bread in this wooden flat box. The more we could place in a box, the more we could take on the road. Get the picture? No bags, no wrapping.

When carrying the bread to the customer from the bread truck, we carried the unwrapped bread in a wooden, wicker basket with a wooden handle, called a bread basket. The expression, "right in the old bread basket" must have originated from us.

The bread route was the life blood of our family business, and as I mentioned many times, Pa, the boy wonder from Verzino, was the master of our bread route. We sold some bread over the counter of our store to the locals, wrapped in brown Kraft paper and tied with twine, but we sold the great majority of our bread through our mobile division, on the road.

Our route started with our best customer, The Gloria Chain Store, an Italian-deli-type store, located on the corner of Rantoul and Federal Streets, in the street-floor storefront of a three-decker house. It sold Italian cold cuts, cheeses, Italian canned foods, fruit, and all types of Italian delicacies, and Columbus bread! We had to deliver there at least three times a day, more on Saturday, to keep the bread warm and fresh for their customers. On Saturday, they generally sold more than two hundred loaves. When a batch of bread came out of the oven, we would immediately bring fifty or so loaves to the Gloria, where there were people waiting. At that time, Spike DiVencenzo, a Beverly man, was the manager, and he considered our bread an important item in the store and gave our product choice locations.

There were also other stores, near or on Rantoul Street, that were very important to us, such as:

Ricci's Market, which we previously referred to many times, was located on the corner of West Dane Street. We were personal friends with the family. Ma bought her meat there because they cut it the way she wanted it cut and they had very good meat. Ma was sort of fussy, and they frowned a little when she entered the store. In the summertime, they sold their homemade Italian ice (gelata, we called it) that was most delicious. Pa and Ma use to buy it for us by the pitcher full when it was too hot to sleep.

Sam's Market was located near Roundy on Rantoul, on our side of Rantoul, two doors down from the corner. The corner building was occupied by Balanger's Candy Store, catering to the Washington School students, and then came Sam's. After Sam, Red Datillo lived in a one-story home with a driveway, covered with grapevines, and next to him was the Whitman Buick dealership, with their repair garage. The only reason we had Sam for a customer was that Frank "Cheecho" Filtranti, our good buddy, was his nephew and lived on the third floor of the store. Sam saw some pictures I drew once and, in his way of encouraging me, he used to pay me to do signs for him.

Pisani Market was located further down Rantoul near Railroad Avenue, around the corner from the train station. They had the market and the next door bar and restaurant. The store was large, with a living area in the rear. Rose Pisani, wife of Mike and mother of many, attended the store and was very sociable. It wasn't long, however, when their daughters took over both establishments.

Simone Acciavardi's Market was located on Elliot Street, down from the drug store on the corner, in the storefront of the Elliot Street Chambers. It was the busiest of all the markets. We didn't get to sell bread there for some time because Simone and Pa had a falling out over the price of our bread and did not speak to each other for years. *(Maybe it was the price of bread, or it could have been "first and second boss." Simone did love his beer and would not have liked going dry ... just kidding.)*

When Simone's daughter took over the management of the market, things were straightened out, and Simone's market became a good product outlet for us.

Govoni's Market was located on Cabot Street, opposite Elliot Street, where the Town and Country Paint and Hardware was, and where the Richdale Convenience Store and parking lot is. The elder Mr. Govoni started the store as a fruit and produce outlet, but the sons, mainly Harry, turned it into one big market that catered to the "well-to-do." It was the first store that I knew of that boasted a complete section of gourmet foods. I had suggested to Harry many times that our bread should be featured in the gourmet food section, but he would only laugh. Harry was the only store manager that had special display bags made for our bread. Pa thought he was nuts; he used to say, "Whoever heard of Italian bread being wrapped."

There were other store outlets, but the above mentioned were the main characters with which we enjoyed great relations, until the supermarkets spoiled all the fun.

After attending to the wholesale end of the business, we had to attend to the retail end, starting in Salem, along Bridge Street to the French area, along La Fayette Street, then into the Italian area, around St. Mary's Church, High Street, and Endicott Street. Then, to Gallows Hill, over the rickety wooden bridge that went over the railroad tracks, and to Canal Street and Bertini's Restaurant, about thirty-two stops in all, and back to Beverly.

Beverly started around the bridge, Goat hill, Porter, Front and Water Streets, around Stone, Union, Lovett, Pleasant, and my favorite stop was to Mr. James Cronin's mother on Pleasant Court. Mr. Cronin was the principal of the Briscoe Junior High School. His mother just loved our bread, and always said, "James just loves your eye-talian bread." The Ryalside area was next.

Up Bridge Street to Winthrop and down by the water, back to Bridge, down Giles, then to Williams. One of the first in Beverly to give his life in the War was the Cappola boy, Anthony, my classmate. The Cappola family was a customer for years, along with many other families in Beverly with teenage kids. I always thought it was "something" to see kids eating their sandwiches in the school cafeteria made with our bread.

Down Davis, and a few stops on Elliot Street, we delivered bread to practically every home on Park Street, then to North Beverly. But first, we had to return to the bakery, reload with bread, and take a break. Before we did this, however, while on Park Street, Pa took out his pipe, loaded it with DiNapoli tobacco, and struck several matches in order to light his pipe—a pipe with one of those bone mouthpieces, bent down to his chin. That took about ten minutes to do. Then, because all our house customers paid by the week, he would take out the account book and go to each customer's name, to see how many loaves the customer took, so that he could mark it down.

The pencil he used was usually a little stub because every two minutes he had to sharpen the point with his jack knife. It took five minutes just to open his jack knife. That whole procedure took another ten minutes, each time he did it. After that, before he wrote a figure down, he wet his finger so that he could more easily turn a page, sucked on the end of the stub to wet down the lead, and then wrote the figure down. He wet his finger again and went through the whole procedure again. Do you wonder why today I am a little impatient with anyone that fiddles and diddles before driving off. I would have to sit in that truck doing this *accounting* for about thirty to forty-five minutes, and getting seconds on that DiNapoli tobacco.

If you know what that tobacco smells like, then you know what I'm talking about. *(Yikes, it drove me craaaaaazy.)*

After we loaded with bread again, we went to North Beverly, not too far up, only to Russell, Windsor, and Jordan. Then, we headed down to Simon, Grant, Mill, Gage, and the Beckford Street area. There were many stops among those streets. We suspected that, at some stops, our bread was the only substance they had to eat. We then moved to the Hardy School area, and all the surrounding streets, and then, would you believe, another accounting, pipe smoking, finger wetting, pencil sucking, page turning, pencil sharpening, pipe filling, match striking, second hand DiNapoli smoking, and *God almighty have mercy on me* session.

Now, it's about four o'clock, and we go back to the bakery and pick up the night club and restaurant French Bread and head for Danvers and Peabody to deliver to the Golden Anchor, Allenhurst, Jimmy's, and several other clubs and restaurants in the area. Monday, Wednesday, and Friday, we also had to go to Beverly Farms.

Pa really built up a very nice business on the road, but it required daily attention and my entire summer vacations, and it was a pain in the *you know what. A*nd that is all I am going to say about our mobile division.

PA KNEW HOW

Supplier knowledge is very important in managing a business. You have to be aware of what your business requires in order to function with a minimum of expense and with the largest profit, and find that happy place. Pa seemed like a natural for that principle. He developed suppliers to function entirely for him, as though he were their only outlet. Whether he did this intentionally or by instinct I do not know, but he did it like a professional. *Having been a professional buyer and procurement manager, I know from whence I speak.*

For instance, he procured his flour, the main ingredient and the largest expense, from Mr. DiFrancesco, who became one of Pa's best friends. During the big depression, sometimes Pa could not pay his flour bill for months, but the flour kept coming in, at a discount. When my brother Luf was born and had to be baptized, it was Mr. DiFrancesco who became Luf's Godfather.

The cold cuts, Abramo Rey products, were the main product sold in our store, and their distributor and main salesman was Mr. Louie Malatesta, who always made Pa his last stop because he liked talking to Pa, playing a few hands of tre sette, and drinking a couple of glasses of wine before he went back to the north end of Boston, where the distributorship was located. Their friendship lasted for years.

For a man that went through only eight years of "reading, riting, and rithmatic," I think our Pa did a very good job at entrepreneurship. I once told him, during his retirement and when we were both in his cellar and I was helping him make the wine, just what exactly my job was, and he could not understand how an owner of a business enterprise could entrust someone else to spend his money.

"Are they crazy," he said.

And I said in reply, "No, Pa, you taught me how, and they are willing to pay me to do what you taught me."

Then, of course, with a big smile, he understood. But, you know, after thinking about it for awhile, I realized how truthful that old saying is, "The older I got, the smarter my father got." How true, how true.

A TRAGEDY STRUCK THE NEIGHBORHOOD

One Sunday morning, I think in 1938, we awoke to the news that our across-the-street neighbor, Henry Carnevale—we called him Eco—was in a fatal accident, but no one knew the details. We all got out of bed to find out.

We soon found out that, late Saturday night, Eco, Lamo Masarella, Lamo's cousin Patsy Masarella, and Babe Bussone were in an accident on Highland Avenue, on the Lynn/Salem line, at a curve on the road they called "deadman's curve." It was one very bad accident, the worst of my lifetime. Patsy, the son of the blacksmith that had his "smithy" on the corner of Park and West Dane, was killed; Babe Bussone sustained serious head injuries; Eco tore up his leg (he walked with a limp the rest of his life); and Lamo also sustained serious head trauma. Lamo, the only one barely old enough to drive, was driving.

The Masarella boys were nephews to "Mariamala," my midwife, and Lamo was the son of the former city solicitor, a prominent Italian/American lawyer. Soon after the accident, they straightened "deadman's curve" (wouldn't you know they would).

Patsy's death was a great shock to the Italian/American community, one that awakened us all to the uncertainty of life. The entire community went into mourning—shades were drawn, radios were stilled, we cried for weeks. It made a difference.

Louie Masarella, Patsy's father, was never the same again. Shortly after the accident, he sold his smithy to his nephew Armando Bussone and went into retirement. Lamo and the Masarella family moved to California, never to be seen again. Babe Bussone remained in Beverly with his family. Eco remained our neighbor and friend. He later earned a doctorate from MIT in physics and became very successful. The accident was one that was long remembered in our community because it was our first fatal accident and the shock was felt in all our homes.

CHRISTMAS WITH THE LAURANZANO FAMILY

When we first came to Beverly and the family was young, Ma did her best to celebrate Christmas. There was a tree, and Ma baked a lot of pastries, cooked a large meal, and put new clothes under the tree for her five young ones, who were too young and unaware to really enjoy the festivities. But as the five grew older and new children were added, they all started to become more aware of the American customs and became more excitable, and Ma and Pa started newer and better customs.

To begin with, Ma did more baking. I don't think there was an Italian pastry that she did not prepare for the holiday. The deep fried little balls of cake that were smothered in honey, which we ate for weeks after the Christmas holiday, were the main ones that I can think of.

When the kids got older, I think about 1928 or so, Christmas really caught hold in our household. Luf was the youngest at the time, and Allie was in charge of Christmas morning. Ma always did the baking and cooking all week long before Christmas. She baked those bow ties with powdered sugar, those little round cake things smothered in honey, Italian cookies, rigotta pies, handmade macaroni, gnocchi, and sundry other things too numerous to remember. Allie took care of the gifts, mostly clothes, but sometimes a toy or two was thrown in.

Pa always brought bags of fruit and goodies from his last bread stop on Christmas Eve, which was usually the Gloria Chain. When he came into the house, late on the eve, we would go through those bags, and we could have anything we wanted. There was gaiety in the house and anticipation of all the good things to come. Remembering those happy, happy times with my Pa and Ma on Christmas Eve, I think that Pa thought of all the times that he and his siblings had nothing, and he was happy that he could give us such joy. I think that's why he brought home all those nice things to eat on Christmas Eve.

Christmas morning, Ma was downstairs cooking, baking, and singing, and all kinds of delicious aromas were coming upstairs to tantalize us, but we could not budge from our beds until Allie got up and said we could. I bet every person knows that feeling on Christmas morning with their parents, but they didn't know it from Allie. Allie liked making us wait, to tantalize us. I thought so at the time, anyhow. I use to throw things at her to get her up, but she would not move, and when she finally did move, she smiled and said, "Lets go get them kids," and she played Santa Claus.

At that time, I loved Allie like no other person I ever loved. Ma would come and laugh with us because we were so happy, and then Ma would go over and put a big kiss on Allie. I can not properly describe how much help Allie was to Ma and how happy Allie always made us feel on Christmas, even when we were older and with our own families. Because of the unfamiliar customs in America and the language difficulty, without Allie, we would not have had complete enjoyment on Christmas. Allie made it complete for us throughout our lives, right up to the day she passed away, and we will always love Allie until the day we pass away. We regarded her as our second mother, and she was able to fulfill this role because she loved Ma so much and she sincerely, always, wanted to help Ma.

We miss you, Allie.

EASTER SUNDAY WITH THE LAURANZANO FAMILY

First thing Ma thought of when preparing for Easter was to buy new clothes for all us kids. Mr. Katz, the traveling haberdasher, did a large business around the neighborhood, at reasonable prices. Ma was not going to be outdone by any of the neighbors when it came to dressing her brood for Easter Sunday morning and sending them off to church for the nine o'clock mass. That happened to be the best time to join the Easter Parade on Cabot Street.

The second preparation was to make and bake Easter Bread for the entire family, which would last for weeks after Easter. Some of the bread would be long, some round, some twists with a colored boiled egg in the midst of twirls. All were coated with eggs and baked in the bakery oven to perfection. Only Ma could make Easter Bread so perfect. Mrs. Papa, the next door neighbor on Chase Street and a good friend to Ma, also used our oven for years to bake her Easter Bread.

The third preparation was the meal she cooked on that day. You wouldn't believe it. Handmade macaroni; sauce with pork, beef, meatballs, and homemade sausages; rigotta pies; frittata with real prosciutto; fried dough in the morning after church—I could go on and on, but I won't because I'm feeling mighty low right now.

It was a family day, and we were all there, with God, and we were happy.

AND THEN THERE WAS TEN

It's the mid–thirties, and we're all growing somewhat and, in some cases, maturing, but that seems to be for the girls only. Ralph, or Luf, as he is commonly called, is growing, and Pa is paying attention to him, and he seems to be in Pa's favor. You really can't blame Pa for that because Luf is growing into a handsome boy, with a clean, friendly, white smile and a friendly attitude. He looks up to Pa and Ma, as he should, and tries to be as helpful to them as possible. He was born in 1926 and is now pushing ten, but it seems like he's going on thirty-two. He is starting to be helpful in the bakery, though at ten, there is not much you can do, but he tries very hard to please everyone, particularly Pa.

To keep up the Lauranzano tradition of broken legs, Luf accompanied his brother Ned to the Beverly Common to practice football, and in the process, Luf got his leg broken. With the improved procedures at the hospital, however, Luf was only laid up for a month. Whether he was treated to vanilla ice cream, *or not*, I do not know, but since vanilla is not his favorite flavor, I doubt that he was given that treatment.

Guido, or Bud, as he was fond of being called, was born in 1929 and is pushing seven years. He and Luf slept in the same bed together, but because Bud was sick a lot, Luf most always has to find somewhere else to sleep, sometimes between Ned and I and sometimes in the sunroom by himself. It seemed like every time Bud got sick, it developed into pneumonia, and Allie would nurse him back to life with advice from Dr. Maiuzzo, our family doctor. Even so, Bud was growing into a handsome son of a gun, even challenging the handsome Luf and his pearly white teeth. Pa's tre sette friends use to call Buddy "Bing Crosby" because of his handsome features and his blond hair. But Bud belonged wholly to Allie, because Allie always believed, and it was probably true, that Bud would have been lost to us if not for her tender, loving care. *This gives us another good reason to love our sister Allie.*

Phyllis, the baby of the family, was born in 1931, and everyone said she resembled Ma. She is fussed over by the girls, but mostly Mary takes care of her when Ma is working. She is pushing four and has pigtails and is everyone's sweetheart. She is like a twin to Asunda Carnevale's youngest, named Susan or Susie. Asunda and Ma were very good friends and had about the same amount of children, *give or take one or two.*

BEVERLY'S ITALIAN/AMERICAN NEIGHBORHOOD

Tell you what. Let's take a walk around Beverly's Italian/American neighborhood in the mid-1930s and see what it was like.

If you come out of our house on West Dane Street and cross Rantoul Street, straight down the hill to Park Street, you have Kelleher's Ice and Coal on both corners. The right side housed the office, the ice house, the pig sties, and the scales. On the other side, the horses and wagons were stored.

Across the street, on the left, was the blacksmith shop, and the right was a lumberyard. Keep walking into a dirt-covered section of West Dane to the railroad tracks. On the right was the lumberyard, on the left was an empty field with Mr. Massa's cows. On the left, again, following the lumberyard, was a grain storage building. When we enter the building, it smells heavily of grain, and for some reason, we never saw anyone working there.

Then, there's the tracks and the control tower and the engine round, for the locomotives. There is a big blackened tree there that never dies that we swing on a rope from. There is a creek under the tree that the Boy Scouts, to earn a badge, build a bridge over, then tear it down and build again, over and over. We play around there a lot— we capture frogs and pollywogs from that creek, and we build rafts and sail on that creek, right under and past the grain warehouse.

When we go back up to Rantoul, we have Ricci's Market on the left corner, and next to Ricci is Donato Fortunato's building, with the door to upstairs in the middle, separating the storefronts. On one side is Polly's Clothing Store and the other side is Fortunato's Barbershop. We got our hair cut by Donato Fortunato practically our whole childhood life until he died, as did Pa every Saturday night, for a shave. The Fortunato family lived upstairs, and they were good friends to the Lauranzano family. Stevie was my play pal.

Next door is a small building that Kransburg Furniture uses for storage, and next door to that, on the corner of Creek Street, was an empty field we used to cross when going to the Ward Three playground, or generally in that direction. It wasn't long, however, before they built a gas station there. On the other corner is Corte's Market, recently moved from across the street. Mr. Corte bought the building after renting across the street for many years, in Renzi's building.

If we go down Creek Street, toward the tracks again, and cross Park Street, on the left is a large three-decker, owned by Louie Masarella, the blacksmith, Patsy's father. There is a large garden in front of the house and a field in the rear, adjacent to the lumber yard, where we played baseball games. At the end of the field is the continuation of the creek that runs under the grain warehouse. Across from the field is a house where Zia Santina lives with Giovanni and the kids. Also across from the field is the home of the Carnevale family, John and Asunda Carnevale and their large family of very talented kids.

John was a big man, much overweight, with a reddish face that indicated high blood pressure. He maintained a farm behind and to the side of the house, about three or four acres, with farm animals like goats, rabbits, chickens, and a big pig kept in a pig sty. When he butchered the pig, he had another one ready to take its place. He always had a pig growing that he would eventually slaughter. In the meantime, when the pig got large enough, it kind of became our pet— we'd name it, ride it, feed it, and watch it die. We were aghast when it was time for the slaughter, but happily, another soon took its place. "Dooby" Carnevale was a playmate at the time, but before he could go out and play on Saturday, he had the task of picking a bushel of grass from across the street for the rabbits, and so, that also became my task. But I digress, back to Rantoul Street.

After Corte's Market there are three triple-decker houses to the corner of Roundy, where Chipman's store stands. Never could figure out what they sold, if anything. Across Roundy is a large apartment building where Joe Ricciardi lived. He was my age, and when we were in Washington School together, I used to go home with him after school, and he played the guitar. Never knew what happened to Joe. Some say he ended up in prison. I do not know that for sure. I hope not.

If we turn left towards the tracks again, past Park Street on the left is the city stables, where the City of Beverly kept all its equipment, supplies, horses, and trucks. On the right of the stables is the Ward Three playground. Just before the playground, on the left, is Eedie Guidi's single family house. Now, let's go back to Rantoul.

After Ricciardi's house, on the corner of Roundy, there are two other smaller, single-unit houses. The Detorres live in one of them. Joe Detorre, the only boy in the family, was a classmate of mine and a football teammate. The Mezza family lives next door to them—Mike, Tony, and Ann. Then is the Abate Memorial Company. Everyone bought their family stone from them. Mr. and Mrs. Abate produced

Peter, a world renowned sculptor. Fernando, the eldest, was helping his father with the stones. On the corner of Elliot Street is Goldberg's Fuel Oil Company. Bernie was the son that eventually took over the business, sold the property, made a lot of money, and retired. He and my brother Joe hung out for a while.

Across on the other side of Elliot is the Davis Drug Store. The Park Street guys used to hang on that corner, in front of the Drug Store. There was Joe Rocci, Sammy Carrato, Bobby Stuart (he married the other Julius girl, Madeline), Biagio Carrato, Chibac Rocci, Al Latini, and Eedie and Minnie Guidi. Over the Drug Store was a rooming house that eventually would burn a whole floor off the building, and where about twenty roomers perished.

Then, there is an empty lot where, soon, the John Giulianni Restaurant would be built and would thrive, where they would serve Italian cuisine and pizzas by the truck load. Eventually, the place burned down and was never rebuilt.

Just before arriving at Gloucester Crossing, there is a small variety store that serves the high school kids well, with candy, ice cream, snacks in general, sodas, and things like pens, pencils, and general supplies for school. It came in handy. On the corner we have Macauley's Drug Store, where the vanilla ice cream came from when I was in the hospital.

Next to Macauley's is the Gloucester Crossing Market and Butcher Shop. I don't know why, but I do not believe we ever tried to sell our bread in there. Next door, next to the tracks, is another shoe repair shop, and then the railroad tracks and the small hut that housed the man who operated the barrier gates. However, those gates did not prevent a tragic collision with a passing train that recently got a well known Italian/American Beverly girl killed.

We'll cross Rantoul Street opposite Macauley's Drug Store, where there is an empty lot, and head back. Now that booze is legal, there is a documented rumor that the well-known Ted Lyons is financing a project that will erect a building in the empty lot that will occupy his package store, with rental space for other enterprises. After the empty lot, there is a Protestant church, and then it is residential until we reach the corner of Chestnut, where the building that housed Titoni's Bakery lies empty. It was bought and sold a few times but nothing seems to stick there. Soon, an automobile agency will open there and become successful. There is nothing next to it going towards Elliot. There is empty space to Chase Street. Later, when dry cleaning becomes popular, a building will be erected this side of Chase to house a dry cleaning enterprise, between Chestnut and Elliot.

Then, of course, you have our beloved Washington School that everyone in Ward Three went to, since 1913. The first day of school, when you walked back into that building, the smell of newly oiled floors always invaded your nostrils. And for years,

Miss Driver, the principal, was always there to greet you with her jingling keys in her hand. It was called the Washington School then, but some later school board renamed the school the Beadle School. And still later, some other know-nothing politician, non Beverlyite mayor sold the school to a drug store chain, which tore the school down to build a drug store on that blessed property. *Politicians have no heart or soul; therefore they cannot think like a human being ... But again, I digress.*

After the school, practically on the same property as the school, on the corner of Roundy, is a local fire station, an old wooden structure that served the city well. Our next door neighbor, Jim Pinciaro, Angelo's brother, is a Beverly fireman who did all his duty at this fire station for many years until he bought a house in Ryalside and transferred to the Ryalside fire station on Bridge Street.

On the next Roundy Street corner is Belanger's Candy Store, which served the school kids with penny candy and inexpensive things. Lou Belanger lived there with his father, mother, brother, and sister. I mention this because Lou became a great Beverly athlete, a first baseman and basketball player. Lou played basketball for the Boston West End Club, the forerunner of the Boston Celtics. He also teamed with his best friend since childhood, the best second baseman the city has ever had, Giulee Scoliotti, who lived on Chase Street; and with another buddy and childhood friend, Mario Pasquarelli (Freddie's brother), corner of Chase and Roundy. The three of them came into the bakery every Friday night for a Columbus Bakery special sandwich. We would cut a whole loaf of bread lengthwise, sprinkle olive oil and put in salami, cappacola, provolone, and whatever else they wanted, and cut it three ways—they paid seventy-five cents and went on their way. I think we started the pizza and submarine sandwich craze in this country, that we do not get the credit for.

Belanger has a side yard, with grass and trees and a garden, that abuts Sam's Market. The market occupies the ground floor of another three-decker house. Our best buddy Cheecho Filtranti lived on the top floor, but he might not be in residence yet from the North End in Boston, where he moved here from.

Then, it's Red Datillo's single residence. I told you about him before. Nice, small house, with a long grapevine over a long driveway. Red was always sitting out front waving at everybody that went by on Rantoul Street. I think, during his younger self, he was a prizefighter, with the resulting configurations and mental disabilities. Good guy, though. Everyone loved him.

One of the very few automobile dealerships in Beverly is next door to Red's place. It's called Whitman's Buick. It's wide open in the front where the previously owned cars sit; the rear of the lot is the repair garage; and perpendicular to the repair shop, in an ell-shape, is the showroom for their new cars. This is where Pa bought his Buick. There is also a repair and paint shop below ground.

Walking forward, there are two three-deckers with no storefronts. The Nadeaus, Saghettis, and Parasillas were a few I remember that lived in these apartments. Ray Nadeau, probably the best basketball player Beverly ever produced, played with the Boston West End Club with Lou Belanger. His brother Charley married Violet Colletti, Beverly's most beautiful Italian/American girl ever. Following is another three-decker with two storefronts. The first store is Vito Cacciolli's Shoe Repair, whose namesake is a bachelor that lives alone in the rear of his shop. We think he was a gay man, but we do not know for certain, so we'll leave it at that. The other store is a little variety store, run by a little old lady who did not do any business that I could see, but she owned the building with her husband, and loved to go dandelion picking every day.

Kransburg Furniture is next. It is the largest business enterprise on the street. It was newly built, with three floors of furniture and two large show windows. The front door is in the center between the two show windows. When I walked into the store, I'd walk up the middle of the store, with tons of furniture on each side, and Harry, Sam, or John Kransburg would be standing around waiting to sell something to someone. The store always reeked of furniture polish, new upholstered furniture, and new leather. It always seemed so homey. The middle aisle brought you smack into their office, where I was always sent to pay our weekly fifty-cent installment payment to Mary DiRubio, their office manager. As a matter of fact, Kransburg had recently introduced the new inlaid linoleum floor covering that Pa immediately had installed in our home on West Dane Street. This act would eventually prove to be a bane on my life. It was installed by their carpet and linoleum installer, Steve DiRubio, brother to Mary and John. Steve worked with the Kransburgs as their installer his whole life, right out of high school. It was the only place he ever worked, and the same with his sister Mary.

There is a driveway that belongs to Kransburg, and then Renzi's building, one storefront with an apartment in the rear of the store, where Frank Corte rented and maintained a store for many years. The Renzi family resides upstairs. There is Renzi and his wife and two daughters. The Renzi daughters were very popular girls in the neighborhood. One was Beatrice, called BJ, who was a teacher in the Beverly school system and married Carmenuch Vitale of Roundy Street. Her sister, Susan, married Nick DiMala, a popular athlete in Beverly. Mr. Renzi was a prominent man in Beverly and owned the store on the first floor before selling to Corte.

Little is known of the small store that follows Renzi's, but I believe that Renzi owns that property also. George Nardella is running a restaurant in that building.

George is the brother of Susan Carnevale on Creek Street. In the near future, however, Pat DiRubio, brother to Steve, John, and Mary, will open a radio repair shop in this building. But I will remember George Nardella's restaurant the most. The aromas emanating from there were s-o-o-o good. Unfortunately for our neighborhood, that very sociable and likable George Nardella died young, and the restaurant could not stay open. The name lived on, however, with his nephew George, my boyhood friend who we called Dooby, who lived on Creek Street, and who owned and ran the Post Office Diner for years. Tragically, he also died young.

Then, of course, next is the second largest business enterprise on Rantoul Street, Kramer's Department Store, on the corner of West Dane Street. I have to preface this by telling you that Kramer built this building, a beautiful building for the time, after buying the corner apartment house and the clothing store owned by a Jewish lady by the name of Polly.

Kramer's new department store was a beauty, competing with the best of Cabot Street, like Almys , Davidson's, or Grants. Polly moved across the street into Fortunato's empty storefront and opened a new clothing store. She would stand out front of her store, and to anyone going into Kramer's Department Store, Polly would yell, "Yoo hoo, I'm over here now." For years afterwards, if anyone in the neighborhood desired the attention of anyone else, they would yell, "Yoo hoo, I'm over here now," imitating Polly. *Poor Polly*. Kramer's Department Store put her out of business soon after, and we never heard of her again. It's too bad because she was on the corner when we moved onto West Dane, and Ma went there often to buy things and they, kind of, became friends.

Across West Dane from Kramer's is the building owned by Mr. and Mrs. Dominic Ricciardi, who live on the second floor of a three-story building, with a storefront and an apartment in the rear of the store. They have a daughter, Veronica, who is one of Fannie's best friends and playmates. The storefront is rented by the Schiarcca family, which maintains a fruit store and lives in the rear apartment.

A small rental house is next door that is rented to Henry Latorella and his wife, Wanda, an Ipswich girl. Wanda had two cute sisters that lived with her, Sophie and Frita. Needless to say, we hung out around there a lot in 1936. Sophie and Frita were just *too perfect*. As it turned out, Sophie, unfortunately, married Gino Pasquarelli and had a miserable life, and that's understated. Frita married Mario Pasquarelli, but she was first engaged to marry Freddie Pasquarelli. When Freddie died tragically, Frita turned to his brother Mario and had a very happy life.

Then comes Lyman's Plumbing Service and Supply. Guy Lyman owned the business that was a rather large plumbing service, and he became wealthy and built a large home on the sea coast, along Dane Street Beach. He hired some of the neighborhood kids and made them into first class plumbers.

We see the Cosby Block Building next, which is almost a block long, with two upper floors holding umpteen apartments, and which is newly built, with the entire street floor having only storefronts. The first one you see is the Blackstone Café, with a sign that proclaims, "Booths For Ladies," with a painted hand pointing to the rear. That is the first time I had ever saw a sign that said anything resembling that. Booths for ladies, indeed!

Then, there is Blackie, the guy that sells work clothes, mostly those overalls with the reinforcing rivets that have recently become so popular. Blackie is a little Jewish man who has a very dark complexion, hence the nickname Blackie. And then ...

The most popular establishment housed in the Cosby Block is The Rantoul Hardware Company, founded and operated by the brothers Oatie and Dave Manual. The interior of the store always has a smell of window putty, oil saturated floors, and new rubber. Oatie and Dave are glaziers and putty is their thing; and they are also merchants, selling everything from nuts to bolts, as they say—but mostly, they will put a window in for you or sell you window glass, cut to size, or even a kitchen sink, *I think*. They do well there because they are so well respected in the community, especially by the Italian/Americans. They competed with Winer Brothers Hardware, a giant hardware enterprise that did business further up the street.

Oatie and Dave are also the founders (and participants) of Beverly's famous Black and White Dance Band, where Oatie played the piano and Dave the trumpet. It truly is black and white—for example, the Manuals are black; while Tony Papa, my back yard neighbor, is white and he played trombone; Guy Allaruzzo, the Ryalside laundry man, was also white, and he played reed; and the band consisted of other black guys and white guys. They would be playing a lot of functions in Beverly for many, many years to come, including my sister Mary's wedding.

There are many more occupied stores in the Cosby Block, too many to mention here, so let's move on to the next door to the Cosby Block, Nick Galluzzi's building, which houses his well known drug store on the corner of Pond Street. Next to Nick's drug store, going back towards the Cosby Block, is Latorella's Fruit Stand, with his great sidewalk fruit displays and always fresh fruit. Mario and Henry, the two sons, worked there with their father. This is followed by Sam Lee's Chinese laundry, where all the elite of Beverly meet to have their shirts laundered and starched. These Chinese guys just scared the hell out of me. I wouldn't go near the place until I was at least fourteen. After that, however, when I started bringing Joe's shirts there, we became very friendly. They would always say, *"Howa Joe, howa Joe?"*

Nick Galluzzi's Drug Store was where everyone in the Italian/ American area of Beverly got their prescription drugs, and their booze on Sunday. Since drug stores, in those days, were allowed automatic liquor licenses for medicinal purposes only, and all bars and package stores were closed on Sundays, Nick saw an opportunity and took it. During prohibition, it was an everyday business venture and an opportunity to sell hard liquor. He built a huge estate on Prospect Hill, overlooking the ocean, and lived happily ever after.

However, Nick was a well respected man in Beverly, and because he fulfilled a need, no one, including my father, bore any resentment towards the man. As far as I'm concerned, he made the best strawberry milkshakes in town, and the largest, and I love him for that. Every time I went into his store for a milkshake, he always said, "Hi, Rico." I guess, being the excellent businessman that he is, he knew I'd grow up one day *... and need a bottle or two.*

Across Pond Street to the next block is another large brick edifice that has a store on the corner occupied by a First National Store—not a superstore, but a popular chain store—managed by Harry Bovio, a well known local figure in town. Harry worked in that store since high school and worked his way up to manager. He proved how smart he was by selling about twelve to fifteen loaves of our bread everyday, double that on Saturday. He and I got along great.

In the rear of the First National, along Pond Street, in the same building but a separate store, there is a Jewish butcher that sells only kosher meats and poultry. Several Jewish families live in the apartments on the upper floor. Next door, Max Rubenstein has a sheet metal shop occupying two storefronts, doing an outlandish business in Beverly and the surrounding communities. He even did work for Pa a couple of times. Upstairs, over the sheet metal shop, is the Beverly Republican Club that Pa, being the good republican that he is, enjoys a membership in, and where they put on some p-r-e-t-t-y good parties. *Boys will be boys, my mother always says.*

After which, there are two more three-decker houses with storefronts. One has a Jewish store where, every day, they sell bushels of bagels that are delivered to them from a Chelsea bakery, owned by a Beverly family by the name of Rantz. (I'm not kidding here.) They have two sons, Barney and Joey. Barney played football for Beverly and married a Beverly girl, Dorothy Frieberg. Pat DiPoalo, a neighbor of ours living on Chase Street, married her sister Elaine. The Rantz family lived on Bennett Street, and when the boys took over the bagel bakery, they continued to do well. The other storefront, the one on the corner of Federal Street, is occupied by yet another Italian cobbler. My cobbler, though, is still my sweetheart, Vito Cacciolli. Cobblers were very popular in those days, *because, in those days, we had shoes repaired!*

Opposite corner is the Lido Market, owned and operated by the Lido brothers. They sell our bread, but not too well. All the Italians call the oldest brother Bagna-olla; why, I don't know—it means bathtub.

I think we'll cross Rantoul Street, which, by the way, is a cobbled street with electric trolley tracks running down the center of the street. The corner store is the Gloria Chain, the Italian-deli-type store that occupies two storefronts. Much was said earlier about this store, so we will just move right along to next door. But before we do, let's walk down Federal Street to Park Street and turn left across Federal to two doors down, where Mayor Torry has his blacksmith shop for so many, many years and that his father had before him. He services all the city horses with new shoes and repairs all the city equipment and wagons. He did not get this work from the city because he was the Mayor of Beverly. Mr. Torry got this work and then became the Mayor.

Now, back to Rantoul, next door to the Gloria Chain, is a building still in the three-floor category, with a storefront. The storefront is home to a barber shop owned and operated by Paul Galluzzi, brother to Nick, the druggist. Mr. Galluzzi has two children, Paul Jr. and Laura. Laura was a classmate of mine through twelve grades. She was a very quiet girl who never seemed happy. If we knew now what we will know later, we might have put a few questions to her, because Laura committed suicide in the single family house, to the right of where Allie and Joanna lived, on Lothrop Street. Laura was a lovely, sweet girl who should have had a long and cherished life, especially since she married so well.

Hey, lets drop in for a beer at the next place of interest, The Venetian Café, at the corner of Riverside Street. This very popular water hole is owned and operated by everyone's friend and father confessor, Fred Paglia. Fred has three children, Minnie, Louie, and Fred Jr. Minnie will marry the gent that will eventually take over the business. They do a nice business there and they will be doing business in Beverly a very long time, so a beer will taste good here.

Hey, what am I talking about! I'm too young to drink! So let's move on to the next, very interesting block.

On the following corner is a glass store selling all kinds of glass, even mirrors and windshields. Next is a single house that is like a revolving door—renters come in and renters go out. Living there now is the twins Ron and Al DiAnni, with their parents and sister. Next is a sort of three-store strip mall. The first store is rented by an Italian tailor who lives on Chase St. His name slips my mind. Well, he died suddenly one day while working in this shop, and Davidson and his daughter Frances took over the tailoring in this location.

Next door is Al DiVencenzo, the popular neighborhood barber. When I grew out of Donato Fortunato, where Pa made us to go while we were little, we became cool guys and went to Al's. Not that this is the last of the DiVencenzos. The next building is the pool hall, owned and operated by the honcho, the big bopper, DiVencenzo himself, the biological father of all the DiVencenzos. He owns the establishment that all the mamas in the Italian area dreaded to see their children hang out at, even though they did, with the exception of the Lauranzano kids *(that is, all but one)*. Everyone called Mr. DiVencenzo "the house," and "the house" created some very good pool sharks in the neighborhood, including our very youngest boy child, Guido.

The only Greek family in the neighborhood owns the next building, where they run yet another grocery store and occupy the rear and the second floor for their living quarters. Theodore, called Teddy, and his brother, Andrew, called Andy, were born and brought up there. Those two kids were partners in gas stations and auto repair garages their entire lives, I mean, until they died of old age. *Stuck together, they did, like brothers always should.*

Next door to the Greek store is the Italian Community Club, which has their facility in a double three-decker house. The club maintains their facilities on either side of the central door that leads to the apartments upstairs. One side of the door is occupied by the bar and community room and the other side is occupied by the function and meeting hall. The rear yard abuts Park Street and faces a tonic company, the North Shore Bottling Company, owned by Bob Albert. This tonic company happens to employ my cousin Jerry Giulebbe as chief bottler and bottle washer. Jerry is very close to our family, more like a brother than a cousin. When my brother Joe isn't working with Pa in the bakery, he goes there to work on a part-time basis. He earns extra money that way. Me and my buds, mostly Stevie Fortunato and Dooby Carnevale, hang out there too. On many occasions, we even earn some money, and we can drink all the soda we want, but you already know, we call it tonic.

Back on Rantoul, next to the club, there is a big wooden building, where they make the springs for mattresses, that is called the Beverly Mattress Company. It stretches for a block, back to Park Street, and at least two lots on Rantoul. A big, brown monstrosity that eats up all the guys in the neighborhood when they can't get hired at "the shoe." No one liked working there, but you have to eat, especially during the depression, when it was difficult to find a job, even at the Beverly Mattress Company.

We are pretty near finished with our walk. I know it has been tedious, but do not fret, relief is in sight.

The next place is a paint outlet and painting company called PF O'Hara Paint Company. There is a big storefront and warehouse in the rear, with a large, wooden plank "drive up" ramp on the side of the store that leads you to the rear of the front building, where the painting division is located and their vehicles are kept.

Then, there is another three-decker house with a storefront that once contained the famous Republican Club, *that Pa is proud to say he is one of their charter members.* In this storefront, the Beverly Republican Club was first located before it moved to larger quarters. At present, half the store is Nuccio's shoe repair, with the other half taken by Petrosino's Barber Shop. On the side of this building, there is a cinder driveway that will lead you to the back yard, where there are two garages, but no cars. They were formerly horse stables, and at present, half the garages are back to being utilized as horse stables for two very cute ponies named Pete and Pat. They are both brown and white and three years old, and are owned by Mr. Reinier, the ice cream man.

Mr. Reinier made ice cream in the little building on the other side of the cinder driveway every summer morning, and in the afternoon, he roamed the streets of Beverly, selling the ice cream. Stevie and I always hitch the ponies and load the ice cream, and when Mr. Reinier returns in the early evening, and sometimes late, we unhitch the team, groom Pete and Pat, and feed them. For compensation, we get to lick the ice cream mixer blades, but honestly, just to serve Pete and Pat was compensation enough. Sometimes, we even get to ride them around the yard.

We loved those two guys.

Then, there is Anastasia's green and grassy yard, a novelty in the neighborhood. Oh ... and what a surprise! They own and operate a store on the corner of West Dane Street, next to Ricci's Market. It is a small convenience store that does not stay in business long—*there are just too many stores.* They have a one-family house that houses six people. Babe is the oldest kid that hangs out on the corner in front of Ricci's Market, and he was one of the guys that brought Fanny home when she was run over by a car.

Thanks, Babe.

And that finishes our walk, aren't you relieved? Now, being very careful not get run over by a car, we will cross cobble-stoned Rantoul Street to go back to our home on West Dane Street. Oh, wait a minute, we have to wait to let an electric trolley car go by—it has just stopped in front of Ricci's store. When the trolley goes on by, we cross the cobble-stoned street, but we see that the trolley stops a little way down because the electric connector rod came off the overhead wires, and the driver is out of the trolley and putting them back together. We continue on, and now we are home, having a refreshment of a cold Puleo's milk and Hostess cupcakes.

I really do hope you enjoyed the walk.

No.1 Pa is shown with his first wife and childhood sweetheart Maria (Leo) Lauranzano in 1909 the year they arrived in this country. Maria passed away a year later in 1910.

No. 2 Colomba Marcucci in 1912 the year she arrived from Fondi, Italy, located on the Almalfi Coast. Poor Ma looks a bit lost.

No 3 Natale Lauranzano in 1909 shortly after he arrived from Verzino, Italy that`s located in the southern part of Italy in the Sila Greca Mountains

No 5 Mary is posing solo on the day of her first communion in her beautiful communion dress. They don`t make dresses like that any more. Is she cute or what.

No 6 The first born of our family but they don`t look it here.
That is Mary(r) and Joanna posing in Fall River in 1917,
just before the birth of Allie.

No. 7 Ma is sitting on Alvira DiPoalo`s front porch on Chase Street
holding Fanny in her lap while Rico is playing near her c1926

No. 8 This is an illustration of our abode and bakery on West Dane Street done by EG Lauranzano (that`s me) to show what it looked like when we were growing up. That`s Ma sweeping the yard, as she often did and Fanny is looking out at her, as she often did.

No 9 The grown up Mary c1932, manager of the store, is holding what must be Guido, because Mary appears to be at least 19 years old. Who else would be that cute?

No 10 The first communion boys Joe(r) and Ned posing formally after their first communion. Those communion suits were handed down to the rest us.

No. 11 Shows the inside of the cave like dwelling in Verzino, Italy where Pa was born in 1878. It is utilized as a storage area at the present time.

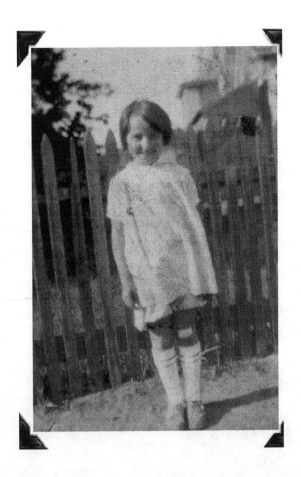

No. 12 Fanny is posing across the street from our house like everyone else and smiling prettily for the camera c1931 at the age of seven. She is cute and always following Ma around.

No.14 Our cousin Concetta (Connie) Marcucci the oldest first generation Marcucci born to Uncle Ralph living in Fall River. Graduation picture in 1931.

No.19 Formal picture of brother Joe and his soon to be wife Laura Maillet from Salem c1938

No. 20 An older Fanny looking through our back door watching Ma sweep the yard. Where Ma was Fanny was sure to be close behind. Get a load of those saddle shoes c1941.

No. 21 Ma is sweeping the yard like she often did. Fanny is looking through the back door talking to her. Ma and Pa liked things neat around the house c1938.

No. 22 Our brother Rafael (Luf) is a young man here c1938, going on 35, born 1926 with the world on his shoulders and he carried it well. You can see Kramer`s Department Store in the background.

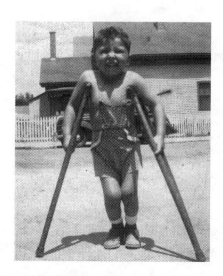

No. 23 Our nephew Paul Pinciaro the first born of Mary and Angelo, probably visiting our West Dane home for Sunday dinner.
Ma insisted they be there every Sunday. A birth defect put Paul on crutches his whole life but he always had a smile for everyone as you can see c1940.

No. 24 Our youngest brother Guido (Buddy) standing in the yard near the one corner of the bakery c1940. The original owner of the pants and sweater Buddy is wearing was Joe and I remember wearing them. We got clothing of our very own on Christmas and Easter. Joe got clothes anytime he felt like it.

No. 25 This is the wedding picture of Freddie Valentine and Mary Rossetti of Lynn. Freddie is second from left and our cousin Jerry Giulebbe is second from right. We show this because of Freddie`s relationship with our family. We were all at the wedding festivities. c1936

No. 26 Our little brother Buddy again and his little dog c1942

No. 27 The top guns Sunday afternoon in our front yard c1939 brother in law, Angelo Pinciaro, Allie and Rico (that`s me) Allie is in charge.

Sporting new jerseys and preparing to launch the 1940 season
From left: Enrico Lauranzano, Aldo Vandi, and Frank Bettencourt

No. 28 Rico on the Beverly football team, that`s me on the left in 1940. Bettencourt on the left was my good friend we almost went into the Marines together

*No 29 Our Pa tending bar at his new bar on Rantoul street c1951
soon to be retired from active work.*

*No. 30 This is the team Rico (that`s me) played on in 1940, I`m front center. This was
taken just before the Thanksgiving Day Salem game in our new uniforms.*

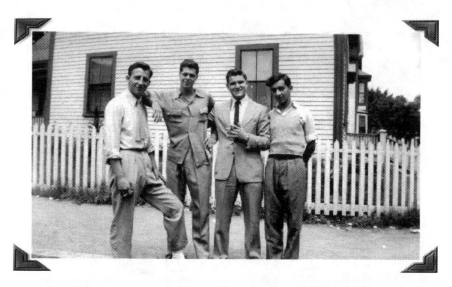

No. 31 A bunch of kids in and around the `hood hung on the corner of Chase and West Dane, on a stoop on the side of the candy store, this is some of them, from left, Rico (that`s me) Guy Allaruzzo, Billy Scotti and Louie Vitale, we called him "Dark Cloud"

No. 32 Ma and Pa sitting together at an early family outing at Chebaco Lake. The outing was sponsored by The Italian Club c1933

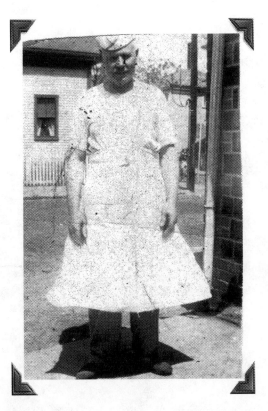

No. 33 Pa in full baker's regalia posing for a picture in the front yard. He didn't usually dress like this he must have been joking around c1938

No.34 Rico's formal graduation picture in 1941 wearing Joe's camel hair sport jacket without his permission. Soon after he gave it to me, maybe he didn't like wearing second hand clothing.

No. 35 Ned`s squad of Engineers in France or Germany c1945 serving in the 7th Army under Lt. General Sandy Patch. Ned is first on the left.

No. 36 Allie and Paul Pinciaro are looking out of the porch window at the picture taking across the street. Ned`s Puerto Rican girl friend is visiting and they are taking pictures of her c1942.

No. 37 And there they are across the street from our house where the sun is better, taking pictures of Ned's girl friend from Puerto Rico where Ned is stationed. From left, baby Natalie, (Mary's second child), Frances, Ma, Ned's girl, Joanna and Phyllis in front.

No. 38 Our two cousins from Newport, on the right is Victor and Hector both home on leave from the Navy, duh. This was taken at the side of their bakery. They are good cousins to us, very friendly and family oriented c1945.

No. 39 Rico, or when this picture was taken I was Rick, and my just wedded bride. In fact this is our wedding picture in Durham, NC just before I shipped overseas with the 89th Division.

No. 40 Our sister PFC Joanna who just got home from the Army on her first leave ever. Our sister Mary, who looks like she just finished driving the delivery truck is greeting her c1945.

No. 41 This is PFC Joanna posing by herself.
She looks good in her uniform

No. 42 Our brother Luf who is home on furlough before overseas duty is enjoying his stay, shown
here with Guy Allaruzzo a `hood friend from the corner. Luf looks proud to be an American.

No. 43 This photo of Rico (that`s me) was taken in Germany at a rest area where I was recuperating and enjoying my stay. Didn`t last too long though Patten beckoned and asked for my return to sleepless nights.

No. 44 Luf in dress uniform taken while he was home on furlough in 1945 just before he returned to duty to accomadate Macarthur's return to the Philippines.

No. 45 Our sisters c1943 Allie and Joanna (sitting) looks like they`re ready to go on
one of their many trips. Together they have practically traveled the world. They`re constantly
traveling together and they have lived together all their lives, real buddies they are.

No. 46 Our brother Luf again in 1945 still on his furlough and still waiting
to help General Macarthur`s return to the Philippines.

No. 47 The three top ones c1943 from the Lauranzano family, from left, Mary, Allie , Joanna and Monica Marcucci (Victor`s wife) on Uncle Guido`s bakery steps in Newport, RI

No. 48 Our sister Frances (Fanny) after taking her final vows to the Sisters of Mercy of Manchester, NH in 1948. She looks so happy.

No. 49 There's our sister Fran again in 1948 up close and looking so nice. We did have a hard time adjusting to her being away from us but her happiness soon won us over

No. 50 The five Lauranzano girls visiting together at the Sister of Mercy mother house in Manchester, NH. The whole family is there we enjoy the visit as an outing. Front is Mary, Allie and Joanna rear is Phyllis and Sister Frances.

51 There is Ma and her good buddy Suzie Carnevale (the Creek Street Carnevales) standing in front of the Greycroft Inn on Dane Street, near the beach, where Suzie cooked and later owned. Suzie had ten children too.

No. 52 Ma is standing in the yard across the street with Angelina Carnevale, sister in law to Suzie. The Carnevale's just bought the house and Ma is there congratulating them. The cherries on their tree will taste just as good.

No. 53 Ma is standing in the Carnevale yard alone now. Angie says," boys please don`t climb my tree I will give you all the cherries you want when they are ripe" But Mrs. Carnevale, we say,"half the fun is climbing the tree"

No. 54 Bud and Alice at their wedding dinner and Bud looking silly (a little like the famous Buddy Holly). That`s Pa on the right and Bud in his uniform then Alice and Allie. You can always depend on Allie to be there when you need someone.

THE LAURANZANO FAMILY

Book II: Growing Up

Our sister Mary is having her long awaited baby in 1936, under the care of Dr. Kidarski at the Beverly Hospital. When the blessed event takes place, we are all excited about the first of our family's second generation. The baby is a boy, and he is named Paul.

Angelo and Mary are living in a duplex on Cabot Street, on the corner of Herrick Street, in the left unit. When the boy is home awhile, Mary keeps noticing that something is obviously wrong with the baby's legs. Her observations result in hundreds of visits to hospitals and specialists all over Boston and further, and after several surgeries, the conclusion is not a happy one. Paul would never walk without help.

This was something all of us had to live with. Mary struggled and "bled" for many years to make this right for Paul, but as before, it was to no avail. It was finally determined, even though it did not make things better, that Dr Kidarski's incompetence was at fault. Even though Paul passed away at a comparatively young age, I have to say to his credit that, given this very hard blow at birth, he made the best of a bad situation and lived his life without regret or self-pity.

You're the man, Paul.

The late thirties see Joe leaving school early and, along with Joanna, starting work in the bakery on a regular basis. Ned and I are attending Junior High School and doing what we can to help in the bakery and on the delivery truck. To Pa's chagrin, however, sports has become a constant in our homestead and a headache to him as well. It seems like every spare minute, Ned and I are organizing a tag football game, stickball baseball contest with bottle caps, street tennis, or just anything that involves a ball.

Our favorite for a long while was tag football with a real football, which we played on our street in front of the bakery and our house, but Mr.Carnevale, who lived across the street in the small house, called the police all the time, and the police would confiscate our football. We lost more footballs that way. Then we got smart and rolled up a couple of flour sacks and tied them together and used the rolled up bags as a football. So, let the police take those. Maybe they could take them home, bleach them, and use them as pillowcases, like many people did in those days. Pa sold them for a nickel a piece.

True to their duty, the police even took the bags, but laughed while doing it, and as soon as the police left, we took out our spare and continued the game. Mr.Carnevale knew when he was beaten and gave up on calling the police. I think—though I do not know for sure—that Pa talked to Mr. Carnevale about his being a bigger pain in the neck then we were.

Ma was good friends with Mrs. Carnevale—Angelina was her name. Those photos you see of Ma standing in a grassy yard are in the Carnevale yard, located across the street from the bakery. I didn't want Ma to have trouble with her because she made the best anise biscotti in the world; and every time she made a batch, she sent some to Ma; and I love homemade biscotti. Luckily for me, before Angelina passed away, she had given the recipe to Ma; then Ma gave it to Allie; Allie gave it to my wife, Frances; and I enjoy Angelina's biscotti to this day.

Growing up, there was always someone hanging on the corner or sitting on the stoop on the side of Florence Starr's corner candy store, to get a game of something going. Nobody was ever lonely in our neighborhood. On Sunday, before we went to the movies, we usually took a walk to Dane Street Beach, and then along the rocks located at the left side of the beach, and then to our secret place that we discovered. Usually it was Bobby Tate, Frank Filtranti, Fred Pasquarelli, Charley Sharp (how did he get in there?), Matt D'allesandro, and me. It had a walled-in garden, imported trees from foreign lands, wide spacious lawns, imported statues, balconies with fancy balustrades—we brought a camera every time we went on this excursion and recorded our discovery that no one else on earth ever saw or even knew about. We would spend Sunday morning there, lazing about, and then go to the movies at the Ware Theater to view the afternoon's first showing.

Some years later, our secret land of enchantment became Beverly's famous Lynch Park, so I guess it was discovered by others while the real discoverers were defending American liberty on foreign lands. *Boy, some people are just ungrateful.*

HIGH SCHOOL FOOTBALL GAMES

Every **Saturday afternoon, we** were regular attendees at the high school football games that were held at Cooney Field. On one side of Cooney Field, on the outside of the field, was a hill, and the other side was the residential side. We had to go early to dig holes under the fence on the residential side in order to sneak into the game near game time. There were cops present, but obviously they had been young at one time and did their own sneaking into the game, so they would turn their backs and pretend not to see us. But sometimes we got a cop that wouldn't turn his back, so we had to climb over the fence on the hill side. That was much tougher to do. I destroyed a pair of pants every time I had to climb the fence when my pants caught on the barbed wire on top of the fence. One way or the other, we got into the game, but my ripped pants did not endear me to Ma.

At the end of the game, we hung around the hot dog stand for the leftover hot dogs that they gave away. On the walk home, we usually raided yards that had apple or pear trees. The old man of the house would come out and chase us away and call us all kinds of unflattering names. They were so selfish about their apple trees, you would think they were going to take their trees with them when they died. Come to think of it, the trees are not there any more, so maybe they did.

One place in particular was on Dane Street, a couple of houses up from Butman Street. There was a well—an old fashioned one, with an old oaken bucket and all—and we always were thirsty from too many green apples, I guess, and we would enter the yard for a drink of that very cold, refreshing water. The guy that lived there must have waited for us, I think, because he would come a running after us, calling us some dirty names that I didn't even know the meaning of, like Dago, Wop, and other nasty sounding names. The first time he did this, I asked Joe what they meant, and he told me, and I never gave that guy that pleasure again. He could have his water; it didn't taste good anyhow.

Those football games in the early thirties featured players that were my heroes—players like Johnnie DiRubio, Charley Pelonzi, Glen Talbot, Nicky DiMala, Peter

Abate. When fullback Peter Abate could not play his entire senior year because he hurt his back, Coach Bodger Carroll put him in the 1932 Salem Thanksgiving Day game, in Salem, as the safety for one play only, and Peter got a standing ovation that I so vividly remember. It lasted for at least fifteen minutes, and they had to stop the game until the ovation stopped. What a great fullback he was. Then there was the little guy that was a big star, Al Harrington, and I remember Zip DiVencenzo, Chibac Rocci, Hank and Mario Latorella, Johnnie Mountain, George Stevens, Hughie Nelson, and many more too numerous to mention here.

The Beverly High School Football Program, how great was that?

JOE BECOMES A FATHER

Betty McGillivray Lauranzano was rushed to the Beverly Hospital July 21, 1938, where she gave birth to a spanking little girl that they named Sandra. When Betty and Sandra came home, we were all over that little gem. Everyone immediately saw the resemblance to Ma because the baby had a mop of black hair and a widow's peak. Ma fell in love with little Sandra and sat with Sandra in her rocking chair by the kitchen window, rocking away for hours and singing her arias to her.

Ma took care of Sandra for a few months because Betty was not well. Then Betty, because of her health, wanted to go home to Gloucester and stay with her mother, and she took Sandra with her. A year or so later, Betty got seriously ill and passed away. After long discussions, Joe consented to allow Sandra to live with her great-grandmother. Joe supported Sandra financially and spiritually, and always recognized Sandra as his daughter. At the time, I guess it seemed like it was the best thing for Sandra, since Ma had too much on her plate, Betty's mother had four other children, and Sandra's great-grandmother was alone and wanted Sandra with her. Joe often said that he was sorry he agreed to the arrangement but had no other choice. Sandra was reared well, grew up, married a man from Minnesota, moved there with him, and raised some very nice children. *Joe, his wife Laura, and their many children still love their Sandra dearly.*

Joe married Laura Millet of Salem. Laura was a pretty French Canadian girl who captured the heart of all us Lauranzanos, and we welcomed her to our family with love and affection. She got along well with my mother and even communicated well with her. She was a Lauranzano now and she seemed happy about it. The wedding was well attended in the French church in Salem, and the reception was at the Italian Community Club. The dancing, eating, and drinking were enjoyed by all. But I have to say, though I enjoyed myself at Joe and Laura's wedding reception, it could not compare to Mary and Angelo's and Ma doing the Tarantella at the Pythian Castle on Federal Street.

ENTER THE FORTIES
THE SHOCK YEARS

The infamous forties—I call them infamous because there was one shock after another for our family, and particularly for Pa. Shortly before getting his diploma from high school, Ned upped and joined the Army. It seems the Lauranzano kids have an aversion to diplomas. That is the first shock that was thrown at us. However, Pa was not as upset as I thought he would be, and I wondered why. I think Pa saw that Ned was often argumentative and disgruntled and concluded that Ned hated working in the bakery, and he decided it might be best for Ned to learn life his own way. So, off Ned went to Puerto Rico and a life of soldiering. Life went on in the Lauranzano household. Even though Ma missed Ned and cried for a while, she did eventually get back to the basics, mainly, the rest of us.

In 1939, close to 1940, I came home late from school one fall day, and Pa wanted to know why I didn't show up to help him on the truck. I replied, "For a while Pa, at least until Thanksgiving Day, I'll be coming home late from school 'cause I have decided it is time for me to play football for dear old Beverly High, the city of your choice." He went literally berserk, and that was the second shock. Pa showed more emotion with my plans to play football than he did over Ned's army enlistment. He threatened to go to the school and prevent me from playing but he never did, and I played that year and the next. He told me later that he stood over my bed at night and listened to my groaning and crying in my sleep, which he attributed to football pain. I told him that I gave out much more pain then I received, and he laughed and accepted that for the time being.

The year 1940 was my year. I was the starting center and I really did distribute pain on an equal basis to everyone playing opposite me. I showed no favorites or mercy *and I took no prisoners*. Looking back on Beverly High football, I think every kid that played and started the games for Beverly got a spiritual high from seeing their name in the starting lineup in the Friday *Beverly Times*, our local newspaper, and I was no exception. In bold letters, they published both starting lineups, with position and weight, and that made you special in Beverly for that weekend. When Pa saw the first lineup, for the Danvers game, printed in the *Times*, he was sold on my playing football and didn't complain again. Of course, Joe and Allie worked on him too.

In those days, football was very important to the Beverly people. On Saturdays, you couldn't get near the field, standing room only. As an example of new interest, Joe was never really into sports or Beverly football until I got into the middle of it, and then, most days, I even saw him at our practices. After we beat Salem for the first time in eighteen years, Joe was the first out of the stands to give me a big hug, and then he and Rocky Papa led the charge in tearing down a goal post and bringing it to Beverly's victory dance. *But it was that hug that really meant a lot to me.*

After every Saturday game, me and my teammates, Frank Bettencourt and Paul Mercaldi, would roam uptown to prance before the girls that hung out in the "Greeks" Ice Cream Parlor. We would also visit my sister Allie at the soda fountain in the five and ten cents store where, win or lose, she would treat us to a coke or two!

DECEMBER 7, 1941

One pleasant Sunday morning in December of 1941, we were about to receive our third shock of the decade. I arose that morning looking forward to the date I had with a girl named Shirley Jones, along with Frank Bettencourt, my teammate and friend, and Deb Debner, his girl of the moment. That day, we drove to Boston in the bread truck and went either to the Metropolitan Theater or the Keith to see and hear a famous swing band—either it was Glen Miller or one of the Dorsey brothers. On the way home, on the truck radio, we heard the devastating news that Japan had bombed Pearl Harbor.

But, you know, at the time, it did not make much of an impression on us because we were busy making an impression on the girls. After all, what's more impressive or important than girls? However, I got a very good idea of what was going on when I got home and heard Pa's emotional description of those Japanese and Germans. So, the third shock was when President Roosevelt declared war. Pa was thinking some very sad thoughts about his sons and their immediate future, outside of his bakery and in the war.

I was a senior in high school at the time, and I was very surprised the next day, when I attended school, to hear that about twelve of my classmates had signed on to go to war. The city was proud of them, it said, and declared it would grant the volunteers their high school diploma and would grant a diploma to any other senior who would volunteer. And others did, which resulted, in some cases, with the supreme sacrifice. Now I started to take this declaration of war very seriously. One of my friends, in fact a teammate of mine by the name of John Dubois, was one of the volunteers. When I asked him why, he looked at me like I had two heads.

I guess you think you know what the next shock is going to be, but you'd be wrong—I do not volunteer now. The shock is actually the third time I total the bread truck. It was on my prom night. I was with Frank Bettencourt, his girl, and Shirley Jones again. We were driving through Wonderland Park in Revere when I sideswiped another car, and it was tow time again. To make matters worse, and to make this incident even a greater shock to Pa, the woman in the other car was *pregnant*! Oh my, this really impressed Pa. Luckily, after the medical examinations that Pa paid for, she was fine, and the baby was fine, and there was no lawsuit resulting from the accident, but it was a shock, nonetheless. Pa stayed angry after this one for a long time. *I guess he was impressed with my ability to sell new Chevrolet Panel Trucks for Naumkeag Chevrolet of Beverly.*

A STEADY JOB FOR RICO

After my graduation from high school, Pa thought I should take over the bread route by myself and offered me the opportunity. I expressed my willingness to do this, but I asked, "What will my pay be?" and Pa replied with a very informative reply, "We'll see." So, without any knowledge of what my compensation would be, I started my job. At the end of the week, when I turned in my Saturday receipts, I asked for my pay, and he gave me two dollars and thought he was overpaying me. Of course, he did not regard the two dollars as my salary—he regarded it as an allowance. Oh well, I didn't need any more than that anyhow. I still ate very good and slept there, so what the heck, who needs more. Also, he was paying for a correspondence art course for me that I liked and appreciated very much, since I had a little talent in that direction, I took the art course very seriously.

My buddy Frank Filtranti worked in Danvers at the Vulcan Electric, where they made soldering irons, and since I delivered to the nightclubs and restaurants in Danvers and Peobody around his quitting time, I usually picked him up after work and drove him home. I know you're not going to believe this, but you probably guessed it— truck accident number four. It occurred after I picked Frank up and we were on our way home. It was in Ryalside, on Bridge Street, just as I went by Kernwood Avenue. I hit a patch of ice, lost control, and banged into a tree—antifreeze all over the street, and it was tow time again. I can still smell the antifreeze, and now, every time I smell antifreeze, I think of that accident. I said to Frank, "Frank, let's join the Army. The Germans will be tame compared to what I'm going to get from my father." But we didn't, and we faced the music, and life went on. That was February of 1942. I guess Pa got tired of bailing me out, because this time he sent Joe to retrieve me and the truck.

MORE SHOCKS

In July of 1942, **Frank Bettencourt** and I decided to join the Marines and went to the recruiting office, where I proceeded to fail the eye test and Frank passed on everything. It was goodbye to Frank. He was now a marine and on his way to Parris Island and some picturesque South Sea islands, and I was back on the bread truck. I didn't see Frank again for six years. He had some problems but he survived.

In August of the same year, Frank Filtranti and I decided to go into the army before we were drafted so we could be given some choices about our assignments within the Armed Forces. We asked for the armored force, because we thought driving tanks would be fun. We were both accepted into the army, but Frank was assigned to the air force and I to the armored force (I guess it was because I drove a panel truck for a living), and we were to report in one week.

So, one night, as Pa was putting bread into the oven, I broke the news to him. You would have thought I was already dead. He started to grind his teeth, and when he did that, you knew there was going to be an eruption. I ducked just as a wooden sawhorse came flying by my head. I guess he thought it was better I died by his hands rather than by the Germans. I made myself scarce and retreated, which was the smart thing to do. The next day, I explained to him that I was going to be drafted anyway, and it was smarter to volunteer, and he reluctantly agreed. Frank and I reported to the recruiting office in the post office, and we were sent to Fort Devens by bus for assignment.

From there, Frank went on to the air force and fifty-one bombing missions over Germany—count them, fifty-one—as a tail gunner. He lost his plane and mates twice over hostile Germany. Frank turned out to become a real, honest to goodness hero. We were all very proud of him and very frightened that we would never see him again. I went to Fort Knox, Kentucky, for my basic training. I was alone in the world for the first time, without my many family members around me. At the age of nineteen, that is a very scary position to be in, I think. I was sad and lonely.

I had thought I was going to be with Frank; we planned to brave it out together, win the war, and go home as heroes. But that was not to be. After I finished my basic training, I thought I was going to go to a tank battalion, train as a tank driver, and go over to Africa and kill some Germans. But that also was not to be. Instead, I stayed in Fort Knox, trained as a tank driver all right, but in lieu of going to an African battalion, I drove officer candidates, also known as ninety-day wonders, through their gunnery courses, week after week and month after month.

One hot summer day, I think it was a Saturday, as I was lazing around the barracks, I received a special delivery letter from my sister Allie advising me of my friend Freddie Pasquarelli's death by drowning. Frank Filtranti was home on furlough, and the two of them went swimming at Obear Park in Ryalside. The undertow got hold of Freddie, and Frank could not save him. I tried to get an emergency leave, I even went to the Red Cross, but because he wasn't family, I just could not get it done.

It was a sad, sad time in my life. Freddie had written to me weekly, and I would miss him and his letters of encouragement very much. He was a very talented writer with a very promising career, and his letters were priceless. Everyone thought very highly of Freddie and his family, and Frank felt very guilty. I don't think he ever got over it. In fact, I always suspected that Frank volunteered for many of his sorties over Germany because of his involvement in Freddie's untimely death. Frank and I continued to correspond, and he wrote of Freddie a lot. I often told him he had to get over it, that accidents happen, but I don't think he ever did.

Still, I'm here to tell you now that Sgt. Frank Filtranti was probably one of the bravest guys of all the thirteen million service personnel of the United States Armed Forces. Fifty-one missions, and shot down twice. *That's my boy.*

And I continued to drive those sniveling, wet nosed officer candidates around Cedar Creek near Elizabethtown while they shot off their cannons. One very cold February Friday, when we finished a week at Cedar Creek, I drove my Sherman Tank to my home motor pool, where I had to wash the tank and grease the bogie wheels. I washed the tank and started to grease it but the foot-pedaling greaser was frozen. I got a blowtorch from the garage, which is the usual procedure to unfreeze the greaser. I lit the torch directly beside the tank, inside the garage, and unbeknownst to me, a mechanic was inside the engine changing the gas filters, which resulted in an explosion and fire. The mechanic jumped out in flames, and others in the garage put his flaming clothes out. I was singed, but not hurt; however, the Sherman had a fresh 155 gallons of high-octane gasoline in its tanks, so they towed it outside and let it burn, and it burned and burned and burned. *You would have thought it was Atlanta all over again.*

Needless to say, there was an inquiry, and needless to say, I didn't tell them of my four bread-truck totals at home. A full colonel interviewed me and came to the conclusion that, even though the mechanic was careless, I still should have been more careful. I asked him for a transfer to a combat battalion or an infantry division and he laughed. *Little did he know what a bomb he had working for him.*

It was maybe six months later, when I was driving a light recon tank on maneuvers and in column formation with a sniveling wet nose in the turret, that the dust became very thick and blocked the daylight and my visibility. We lost sight of the tank in front of us and we plowed over a small cliff, turning the tank over several times. Luckily, the wet nose fell clear of the tank and was unhurt. I was hospitalized, and the tank was a junk heap.

Guess what? When I reported back for duty three months later, I discovered that I was transferred to a Corps Headquarters at Fort DuPont in Delaware to await reassignment. Friends, this isn't what you think. I wasn't getting the boot—the tank gunnery school broke up while I was in the hospital and everyone was reassigned. At Fort DuPont, they informed me that a tank battalion was forming, which most went to, and the 89th Infantry Division was also forming at Camp Butner, NC—which did I prefer? I immediately told them the infantry division. Imagine what would happen to me in a tank battalion. I was already Germany's best tank driver—I was expecting the Iron Cross from them at any time, and I wanted to do something positive for the USA for a change.

Seriously though, please stop laughing. Even though I caused some damage to a couple of tanks, I really was a good driver. One year, I was selected by the school and gave a driving demonstration in the infield at Churchill Downs during the Kentucky Derby. How good is that?

While at Fort DuPont, I didn't have much to do, so I went into Wilmington quite often for some "recreation." One day, another guy, also awaiting assignment, said he knew a girl in Wilmington he thought I would like to meet who was the best friend to his girl. So, I went with him and met Frances Catherine Grothaus, the mother of my children. *Can you believe the way things happen?*

WHAT'S GOING ON AT HOME?

When I went into the service, my sister Mary came out of retirement, so to speak, and took over my job delivering bread. It was very rare in those days to see a woman driving, let alone a truck. I might add that she did this for a couple of years without as much as a scratch to the truck. But she also did this job for a full salary of forty-five dollars a week. Not much when you consider what she could have made as a Rosie the Riveter, but she was family, and the job had to be done, and she did it without complaining.

The bakery saw the return of Uncle John, as he was now called in lieu of the Italian version, Giovanni. This was his fourth hitch, and he was really needed this time. Working in the bakery with him was Luf (Raphael), Bud (Guido), Jenny (Geninna), Joe, and Pa. (Incidentally, at this time, Jenny was in the process of changing her name to Joanna—after all these years, she couldn't stand the sound of Jenny—so from here on, she will be referred to as Joanna.) It seems like a lot of personnel for the bakery, but there was a war on, and changes will come, and changes came.

Joanna and Luf joined the army in early 1945. Luf quit school and joined up just in time for MacArthur's return to the Philippines, and Joanna went to Fort Myers in Maryland for the duration. Luf got to see the Philippines and its jungle scenery and to meet a Japanese soldier on a personal basis when the Japanese soldier gave Luf a Purple Heart decoration—he was a sniper that got Luf in his sights and grazed Luf's head. Thank God his aim was off a little. Luf rolled down a hill after he was hit and his Jap friend didn't get another shot at him. Luf laid there for quite some time before they found him.

When Luf came home and was discharged from the army, he made up for dropping out of school. He received his high school diploma from Neumann Prep in Boston and then went on to earn an undergraduate degree from Boston University and a master's degree from Columbia University. He became a schoolteacher in the

Big Apple, teaching underprivileged high school students the English language. We are very proud of Luf, who now says his real name is Rafael. *Go figure!*

Joe, the chief cook and bottle washer in the bakery, wanted to do his part, too. He did not believe baking Italian bread was helping to win the war. In his spare time, he attended welding classes at Louie Masarella's blacksmith shop, on Park Street. The Navy Yards in the area were short on welders and the government was compensating Louie to teach welding in his blacksmith place of business. Rocky Papa accompanied Joe, and they both learned the craft and proceeded to acquire jobs building submarines in the Portsmouth Navy Yard in New Hampshire—and, NO, they did not work on the USS Squalus. For people who have never heard of the Squalus, it was christened at Portsmouth in 1939, rolled down the tracks to the water, sailed to the middle of the harbor, and sank to the bottom with all hands. They tried endlessly to bring it up with pontoons and all, but never could.

So, that leaves Pa, Ma, Uncle John, Mary, and fourteen-yearold baby brother Bud, who managed to leave his hand in the dough press and was out of action for quite some time. And of course, Bud kept his hand, maimed or not, in the pool hall on Rantoul Street with his friends. He, at least, graduated from high school and eventually went to college. As I said earlier, Bud was such a handsome boy that some of Pa's friends in the barroom called him Bing Crosby, because he had blond hair and was so cute. He was cute, but he was also a worker who was not afraid of work (*he would lie down beside it and go right to sleep*). Seriously, though, he helped Pa as much as he could with the many duties that had to be performed in the bakery while the bulk of the family was out in the crazy, mixed-up world, worrying the hell out of Ma and Pa. *Good boy was Bud.*

THE EUROPEAN THEATER OF OPERATIONS

Why do you suppose a place of war and death is called a theater and a battle is called an operation? I always wondered about that. Well, anyhow, after I courted Frances Catherine for a week or two in Wilmington, then I started to court the dear lady long distance from Durham, NC. I was once again in training, but this time as an infantryman, otherwise known as a rifleman or foot soldier. This was in the fall of 1945, when I also proposed marriage to Frances Catherine and she accepted, although I don't know why. We were married in Durham on the eve of Christmas Day, and a week later I was sent overseas with the 89th.

We landed in La Havre, France, debarked from the lousy ship— and I mean that literally—and trucked to Camp Lucky Strike, a tent city near La Havre. We were the first to stay in this luxury city, and we pretty near froze to death. And if that wasn't enough, we pretty near starved to death. We went out to the surrounding area and begged food from a starving population of French people that happily shared what little they had, particularly their daily bread ration and hot café, and even killed a rabbit or two for us. With no heat in our tents, we woke up each morning with frost in our eyes and icicle growth from our drooling mouths. Why was I being punished? Was this the army's way of punishing me for destroying two tanks?

But I think the camp was not ready for personnel because it was actually being set up to process troops for transfer to the Pacific and the invasion of Japan, and we arrived there by mistake. Our food supply finally arrived from England, where it had correctly been shipped, and our tent stoves finally arrived, and the French citizens from the surrounding area of La Havre, who were so generous with their food when we were in need, ate real well while we were there, and dressed warmly, but we were not there for long. We moved out one cold night in cattle trucks, and four hours later, we arrived at the head of General Patton's infamous Third Army.

When we arrived at our destination, we had to jump off the trucks. Our feet were numb with the cold, our bodies stiff with frost, there was no feeling in our hands, our eyes were frozen shut, and when we jumped down off the truck, about six feet high, we broke into little pieces. Just kidding, we really didn't. However, some of the guys fell when they jumped and could not get up and *did* land in a field hospital, and I'm not kidding about that. We then were assigned to billets to thaw, and we slept our first sleep at the front, to the sound of pounding cannons.

In the morning, we commenced our march to victory with Patton's army of tanks *behind* us, with the end of the war near. I could say here that my presence in Europe ended the war a lot faster than it otherwise would have, but I'd be lying. Still, three months of chasing Germans across some of France and a lot of Germany was an experience one does not soon forget.

You would think that, now that I was out of the tanks, I could stay out of trouble, now wouldn't you? If you think that, you would be wrong. We were in our first—our very first—skirmish with the German Army at a railroad yard somewhere near the Mosselle River. We, in the railroad yard, and they, the Germans, in an adjoining wooded area, were shooting at each other. Our platoon leader was hit in the groin area and was screaming for his mother. Since this was our baptism of fire, it all seemed very strange and, I might add, a little scary—well okay, a lot scary! After firing away and not knowing who or what I was firing at, a white flag went up and we went over to their area and collected this fierce army. Well, we were still a bit steamed up about our platoon leader, so when we were lining these guys up to march out and I saw a medal on one of them that had a profile of Hitler on it, I ripped it off his uniform and threw it. Wow, what a gallant and brave action that was! The medal flew through the air and hit our regimental commander, a full colonel, on his leg. The German soldier screamed that his Geneva rights were violated, and our full colonel agreed, and I was placed under arrest, pending a general court martial. *I kid you not.*

They took my rifle from me; my best friend Don Wingard, the best man at my wedding, was assigned to guard me; and for three weeks, I went through several hot times without a rifle and with Don dogging me. After three weeks, Lieutenant Hanson told me that the colonel dropped the charges and I could go back to full duty.

What a pain that was. I walked all over Germany after that, and sometimes I even wished for a tank. Can you believe it? It is ironic, though, that when I personally heard that the war was over, I was sitting on a Sherman tank, talking over old times with the driver.

All the time I was in Europe, I received a letter from Frances Catherine written every single day. Maybe they didn't get delivered every day, so I would receive them in bunches. Allie also wrote faithfully at least once a week, and the packages from Allie just kept rolling in. Those packages made me one very popular boy. A whole salami, pepperoni, homemade Italian biscotti, and the list goes on.

When we started the occupation of Germany, I was sent back to Lucky Strike to process for the invasion of Japan that proved unnecessary after Hiroshima and Nagasaki, so in lieu of Japan, I was drafted onto the division football team. I played all over Europe and had a lot of fun. Some of the opposing players who didn't get hurt during the hostilities finally did.

Ned was also in Europe as an army engineer, building bridges and stuff down in the southern part of France in the Seventh Army, which was commanded by Lt. Gen. "Sandy" Patch. He was processed for home and arrived home before I did, as did brother Luf. Who said life was fair? Tell you the truth, though, I did almost reenlist when they promised me a furlough of thirty days, with permission to go to Italia and visit Verzino and Fondi. Football players do get their privileges. They even offered me the loan of a Jeep. Frances Catherine won out, however, and I went home and got my honorable discharge. But I was worried, before I got my discharge papers, that they were going to bill me for the tanks because the corporal that processed me out asked me about them. *"Hey fella, what happened with the tanks, ha, ha?" Very funny, Corporal, no wonder you never made sergeant.*

HOME AT LAST

I came home from Europe, landing at a New York pier, and got processed at Fort Dix in New Jersey. After processing, a buddy of mine invited me to go home with him to New York's East Side. There were welcome-home banners for him all over the street. He lived in one of those walkup flats that you always see in those gangster movies, where he lived with his large Italian family. I enjoyed a delicious Italian meal, with all the trimmings, with his family and all his relatives.

After the meal and the goodbyes, I went home by train, and waiting for me at the Beverly train station was Allie, my ever faithful and loving sister, and Frances Catherine, my new bride. There were no welcome-home banners. I wonder, do the New Yorkers love theirs more than we love ours? Well, he deserved all the attention he got 'cause he saved my life once, as he did for several others. He was awarded the Silver Star. Nice kid. We met several times after discharge, but then the trail got cold. I hope that Sgt. James Giametti is well and that he remembers the good times we had together. Like the times we confiscated the wine in those German wine cellars. We made sure the Germans didn't come home to the wine cellars they left behind.

The family was together again, everyone was happy, and Frances Catherine seemed to be getting along well with the family. But we had to find a place of our own to live and raise a family. Frances kept her job with DuPont by arranging a transfer to the Boston office, and I was unemployed, as were a gazillion others coming home from the wars, until Joe offered me a job delivering bread. *What a surprise!* I took the job "until something better comes along."

Mary and Angelo bought a duplex at 22 Judson Street and let us rent one side while they lived on the other. Pa and Ma bought furniture for us as a wedding present. In 1949, I enrolled at the Vesper George School of Art in the Back Bay of Boston and started my art studies, fulltime, under the GI Bill. I took part-time work Saturdays on the bread truck, and at night, I ushered at the Ware Theater.

Joe and Laura lived on Chase Street, right near the bakery, and he seemed to be managing the bakery for Pa. I guess in order to get him back from the Navy Yard and his newly acquired welding career, Pa had to make concessions. Joe was a good baker and businessman, so in my opinion, Pa's choice was sound.

Luf started his schooling on the GI Bill and was going into Boston every day. Ned worked in the bakery with Joe and still didn't like it, and eventually joined the Beverly Police Department and raised himself to the rank of lieutenant. He also married Doris Hawes, a Gloucester girl, and raised a family—one girl, Nancy; and four boys, Natale III, Dennis, Robert, and one stepson, Aubrey Hawes. In later years, Nancy changed her name to Nancel. *What gives here?*

Joe and Laura (Maillet) also raised some very beautiful daughters—Linda, Mary Jane, Laura Jean, and Dianne. Joe and Laura bought a home in North Beverly on Russell Street, where they raised the children and where Laura still lives today.

The decade of shock is still upon us, in case you haven't noticed. It is the year 1946, and Pa received one bad shocker this time. I was in the bar doing nothing one Sunday morning, where our only phone is a pay phone, and I received a call from Italy advising that Pa's older brother Giuseppe Michele had passed away. I called Pa to the phone hurriedly and, half-dressed, he received the news personally. It was very sad, especially since I think Pa thought he would eventually return to Verzino and once again see his brother Giuseppe Michele, but that also was not to be.

In 1946, after I accepted the job with Joe, my bride, Frances Catherine, was having second thoughts about leaving her three younger sisters back in Wilmington in the care of her widowed mother. Her mother, along with her newly acquired husband, was not showing too much concern for the girls' welfare—resulting in numerous complaints from relatives and friends. Out of concern for Frances Catherine's mental health, I quit the bread truck yet again, and we moved to Wilmington to resolve the situation. Frances transferred back to DuPont's Wilmington office, and I got a job in town as a window dresser, putting my artistic eye to work. I attended the Philadelphia Museum of Fine Arts School at night.

It took us about a year, but we finally resolved the sister situation by getting a court order for their care, and we brought them back to Beverly as our court appointed wards—Betty, Marie, and Patricia, ages ten, eight, and six. While we were living that year in Wilmington, in 1947, Frances Catherine gave birth to our first born, named Richard Alan. Then, in 1951, while living in Beverly in our starter home on Chase Street, Frances gave birth to our only daughter, Judith Ann.

In 1952, when I graduated from art school in Boston after four years, I accepted a job as a draftsman—not the visual position that I wanted but a job nonetheless, earning seventy-five dollars a week. We purchased a home in the Beverly Cove area on Woodbury Drive, a new street with postwar new homes for $14,500, and no bargain at the time. Then Kenneth came along and Thomas right after, and that completed our family portrait.

In the Year of our Lord 1948, back in Beverly, my sister Fanny, who we now call Frances or Fran (a more grownup name, don't you know), gave Pa his last shock of the infamous decade. While Pa was having his dinner one fine day in the kitchen of our family home on West Dane Street, Frances bravely informed him and Ma that she was entering the Sisters of Mercy Convent in Manchester, New Hampshire. "You would have thought I took out a gun and committed suicide right in front of him, the way he carried on," Fran told me later. "Ma started crying mostly because Pa was so upset and there just was no talking to him." I told Fran that she should have been there when I told Pa I enlisted in an army that was at war, and how I managed to prevent my head from complete decapitation by ducking just in time.

Eventually, like with everything else Pa at first did not care for, Pa got used to the idea of his daughter being a bride of Jesus, and we had some very nice family visits through the years with Sister Marie Antoinette, the name she took at first when she entered the order. Sister Frances, as she is now known, is retired from active work, has just completed her 60th year as a Sister of Mercy, and is still as happy as can be.

You know, I can still remember when we were both in high school and Fran used to cook a steak for me every Saturday morning before a Beverly football game, "to give you the strength you need," she used to say. Other times, when I'd lend my football sweater to a girl to wear, she used to get it from them and give it back to me. I'd say, "Fran, what are you doing?" And she would reply, in no uncertain terms, "No one wears that sweater but my brother." And you know, I accepted that because she was so important to me. Thank you, Fran, you always looked out for me, and I love you dearly.

PA RETIRES
(CAN YOU BELIEVE IT)

Pa retired from the bakery in 1947 or 1948 and turned the business over to Joe and Joanna for an affordable price. Joe and Joanna made a very unlikely partnership that was most probably not going to endure. Both deserved the business because both put in a great deal of their time in the bakery. But alas, it was not to be, and Joe ended up the buyer and Joanna the seller, and Pa stayed out of it.

A year or two after selling the bakery, Pa was going on seventy–two, with a lot of water under the old bridge, so he started to seriously talk about selling the bar and pizzeria also, and he had gotten a pretty good offer for the business and the building. After the war, remember, Pa had moved the pizza and beer business to Rantoul and Creek Street, where he bought the building from Frank Corte, who ran a store there. The new Columbus Pizzeria and Ristorante was born, with Ma in the kitchen, offering a full menu of her delicious recipes, and Pa in front, with a newly acquired full liquor license, tending bar and welcoming the public. This was the beginning of a real Mom and Pop business in the making. I'll tell you the truth, though, every day at noontime, lines began to form out in front of the place for a taste of Ma's cooking, and because of that, it ceased being fun for her. She thought she was going to cook a few pasta dishes for her friends, collect a half a buck per serving, and be happy. But when that did not happen, it started getting on her nerves and she quit. They went back to just making pizza and pasta dishes, and the crowds started to get normal again.

I usually helped tend bar here for Pa when I got home from my art classes in Boston, figuring he would put the free time to good use. But instead, he used it "wisely," playing tre sette and boss and second boss with his buddies and free loaders. Heck, he was getting up in years and he worked hard all his life, and he deserved some enjoyment. So beware, friends, he is a demon at playing first and second boss, and he takes no prisoners, as I'm sure you have already discovered.

Now, Pa didn't really want to sell because he wanted to leave the pizzeria and bar to his heirs, but we all advised him to go to it, sell the place, and buy a retirement home in Florida so that he and Ma could enjoy life in the sun, away from these cold, blustery New England winters. Pa took our advice, a miracle in itself. He bought a home in Vero Beach, Florida, and he and Ma became snowbirds from 1950 to1957. The only thing disturbing about this was that they both refused to fly like any decent snowbird would do; they took a bus to and fro, and it really wore them down. Plus, Ma's beloved brothers, Ralph and Guido, who were also retired, were constant guests and became very bothersome, especially to Pa.

The apartment on the second floor, over the restaurant, was rented by Ned after he married Doris Hawes and while he was working on the police force. In or around 1952, he bought a home in North Beverly, on Raymond Avenue, and the kids started coming, and that's where he and Doris raised their family.

THE MEZZOGIORNO AND VERZINO
BACK TO ITALIA

Up until 1950, the south of Italy, and especially the mountain areas like Verzino, were still in the hands of a relatively small number of wealthy landowners who were opposed to any improvement in the conditions of their land, tenants, or laborers. The political party that founded the new democratic republic in Italia agreed that a solution to this Southern Problem had to be found because it was the most pressing problem facing the new, postwar Italia. These concerns also were shared by the U.S. political and economic administration, and thus the Mezzogiorno, Italia's poor southern region, was to become the largest Marshall-Plan-funded rural development in postwar Europe.

Verzino and the whole of southern Italia experienced great change, starting in 1950 in the Mezzogiorno, with the establishment of the Cassa per il Mezzogiorno, a development fund for the south. It was established as a separate ministry of the Italian government in 1950 to stimulate social and economic development in the Mezzogiorno, which means midday in Italian (as a reference to the strength of the midday sun in southern Italy). The Mezzogiorno consists of Compania (Naples), Molise, Puglia, Basilicata, Calabria, Sicily, and Sardinia.

Italia's attention to the south was long overdue. For too many years, the Italian government ignored the south. Now, it was experiencing a facelift, with the aid of the Marshall Plan, that would rejoin Italia as one country. The unpaved roads in Verzino and elsewhere were getting paved with asphalt. The government authorized and financed all the necessary new roads that circled down the mountain, in lieu of the eroded dirt roads that led directly down from Verzino and all the other surrounding mountain towns. Highways did not stop at Naples any longer; but went all the way through to the south. Erosion of land was corrected, and even new farmhouses were erected. Arable land was made available to the former peons of southern Italia, and farming machinery was also made available to them.

Industry moved into Bari and Toranto, affording employment to thousands of southerners. Fiat was given financial aid to move assembly plants to the south. The capital of the Province of Contanzaro, in the region of Calabria, was moved from Consenza to Crotone. There, a high school was built that Verzino children were able to attend by being driven there in their newly acquired buses that traveled to each and every town and transported them over the newly built asphalt paved roads that led down the mountain every morning to Crotone. The Verzino children and others in every southern villa were now able to graduate high school instead of being limited to the eighth grade. This encouraged the children not only to graduate high school but also to go on to even higher education, and many of them did with state-sponsored scholarships. Essentially, the Mezzogiorno development and stimulus program changed Italy from two Italias to one Italia, with equal attention to the south, as well as to the north.

Our clan was also growing in Verzino, as well as in Beverly. With the passing of Pa's older brother, the senior Giuseppe Michele, his son Natale, who was called "Pepe" by everyone, became the patriarch of the Verzino end of the Lauranzano family. Pepe had four children with his wife, Luigina Clausi (deceased)—Michele, born 1942; Filomena, born 1945; Carolina, born 1948; and Francisco, born 1951. Pepe had control of Pa's olive grove, and he also eventually remarried. The generation that belongs to Pepe's grandchildren would be the real beneficiaries of the Mezzogiorno stimulus. All of them, excluding no one, would go to university or to a school to learn a trade. One of his grandchildren is on the way to becoming a medical doctor, another is a biologist, another is studying architecture, yet another is a dental technician, and the kudos go on and on. *How good is that!*

Since Pa was now a retired gentleman, Joe talked him into taking a trip with him to Italy. This was in 1954. Joe's plan was to go by ship so that he could take his new Buick with him, drop Pa off in Verzino, tour Italy and France, and return in three months to pick Pa up and bring him home by ship again. Pa agreed to the plan, and we thought, surely, that we would never see either one ever again.

The day arrived. Joe had his car put aboard, and he and Pa joined it, and they departed for the Old World. Pa finally arrived back in Verzino after being away for forty-five years, as Joe put it, "quietly and subdued, like he was just returning home from the store after purchasing a quart of milk." He stayed in the very same house from which he originally left in 1909, and he slept in the same bedroom that he and Maria occupied some forty-five years ago. One thing, though—he could not tolerate not having an indoor bathroom, so he had one built, plumbing and all. He went down mountain and contracted for it, had the material delivered, and built the bathroom with the guy he hired from down mountain. To this day, the Verzino relatives will point this out to any Lauranzano visitor from America, "This is the bathroom that ..."

Joe said that the Verzino people hardly ever saw a car, especially a new Buick; and he had to give everyone a ride when he arrived and, again, before they left for home. He said it was difficult with Cousin Tommasina because she weighed some three hundred or so pounds and was the most excited about the car and about seeing her Uncle Natale. Joe also told us how difficult it was to drive his large car up and down the mountain; in fact, at times, he said, he didn't think he was going to make it at all. It took about three hours to travel one mile above sea level over an eroded dirt road. Of course, this was before the Mezzogiorno Stimulus Fund became a reality in Verzino.

Our cousins Salvatore Iaquinta and Domenico Tallerico told me countless times how they sat with Pa every day in the town plaza and how sad Pa was when he told his nephews several times that he could not imagine that any of his children would ever visit Verzino because they just do not have the interest. They told me this when I was presenting their library with my rendition of the Chiesa Madre (their church) in memory of my father, Natale Lauranzano. They had me in tears when they said how proud he would have been with this gesture in his honor. But of course, by then, several children had been there to visit their Italian cousins, including grandchildren. Allie was always in touch with them throughout her life, and now Robin, our loving niece, is taking over and will not let our relationship with the old country die.

Oh yes, I believe he would have been very proud of all of us, so don't let the trail get cold, Robin.

PA CONTINUES HIS RETIREMENT

When Pa returned from Italia and Verzino, he had many stories to tell, but you had to prod him to tell you anything. Luf sat with him and sort of gave him a Cronkite treatment and questioned him endlessly about his visit and his whole life in general, and they intelligently put it all on tape. But alas, Luf lost the tape and all was lost. *Well, some things were lost, but other things were cemented in my memory, never to be lost, and that is, after all, the reason for this narrative. But I digress ...*

Bud had graduated from high school in 1947 and joined the air force in 1948. What was that all about? After basic training, he was stationed near Columbia, SC. At the time Bud enlisted, he was keeping steady company with a very pretty gal from Rockport, Mass., which is near Gloucester, by the name of Alice Palmquist. He proposed to her, and she accepted, and they got themselves hitched in Columbia, with Pa, Ma, and Allie as their witnesses, as well as Uncle Ralph, who was visiting Ma and Pa at the time. After the ceremony, they had a big dinner at a local eatery. A few glasses were enjoyed by all, after which Alice stayed with Bud until he shipped out to duty in Germany and then went home to Rockport to continue her nursing career.

Back in Beverly, as I stated previously, Mary and Angelo lived on Judson Street with their three children—besides the previously mentioned firstborn, Paul, who died relatively young after his valiant life, there was Natalie and Alan. Most important at the time was that they owned the only television set in the family. Every Sunday, we all would gather at Mary's and watch Ed Sullivan's *Toast of the Town*. On other occasions, we would visit Mary to watch Jackie Gleason and, still other times, to watch Sid Caesar and Milton Berle. Mary must have loved all the company because she never complained.

Eventually, Mary and Angelo bought a house in Centerville on Hull Street, which came with an extra lot of land where Angelo built an outdoor barbecue. You know how our family loves picnics and outings? Now Angelo and Mary introduced something new to the family formula—COOKOUTS! Mostly every Sunday for a while, we had a cookout at Mary's, and then it cooled down to holidays and special occasions. Sometimes, we even had lobster cookouts. *How good is that?* The family group kept getting larger by the year, with kids getting older and new births occurring almost daily. When Mary announced a family cookout for a Sunday, she never knew how many active guests would show up. We had a lot of fun in Centerville, and Mary enjoyed doing it for us. She loved being the "hostess with the mostest," and we enjoyed her doing it. *God love you, Mary, and keep you by his side.*

In 1952, Bud came out of the service and joined his bride, Alice. They started out by renting an apartment on Beckford Street and having their first boy child, who they named Michael. Not long after that, they saw Christopher come into their lives. These two were like twins and very competitive, as youngsters have a tendency to be. They finished out with Robin, their only girl, and then their youngest, Marco. They bought a home on Butman Street that abuts the Beverly Central Cemetery and brought their children up there.

This is the part I have been trying to avoid, but I can't avoid it forever no matter how hard I try. It was in 1957, on a Saturday afternoon. Pa was not doing anything, and it wasn't quite time to go to Florida. He got a ride from Allie or Joanna to the bakery from Dartmouth Street in North Beverly, where he and Ma were living at the time, because he thought the bakery gutters needed cleaning. When he got to the bakery, he hefted a big, heavy ladder out of the garage and placed it against the bakery, and when he did that, he got a pain in his chest and went home, and they put him to bed, and he got another pain, and they called for an ambulance, but he was already gone when they got there. When I was notified, I sped there, but when I got to the house, I met Zip DiVencenzo, a friend and a policeman who was on ambulance duty, and he shook his head to me, and I knew then that I lost my friend and father.

Joe, who was very close to Pa, was on vacation at the time and could not be reached. He was somewhere in the wilderness fishing or whatever, and we had no way to notify him. It was a three-day wake, and on the second day, Joe came home and found out about Pa the hard way. We feared the worst, but everything worked out for him, I think.

We procured the twenty-four-grave family plot at Saint Mary's Cemetery on Brimbal Avenue, and Pa was the first to occupy it. The stone for our plot was designed and made by Abate and Sons, and the plot is now getting more populated as each year goes by. But if anyone is interested, that is where we will *all* be eventually. *If you want to swing by and say "hi" sometime, we would appreciate it. You might not be able to see our smile, but you can be sure it will be there.*

You know, as I write this narrative, I keep thinking that it would be very similar to any other first generation Italian/American writing about their family. Italian/American families are much alike in many ways, and that's why I think Italian/Americans of the first generation feel a kindred to one another. When an Italian/American became a celebrity, like Joe DiMaggio, Frank Sinatra, or Perry Como, for example, you felt you knew them personally because they grew up with essentially the same mother and father, with the same concerns and problems. We all had a mother that cooked the same foods, and spoke to you in the same broken English or in Italian, and showed their love in the same way. One time, I met Joe DiMaggio at a benefit for Red Sox player Tony Conigliaro, after his stroke, and he told me the very same thing. He said that every Italian/American mother or father he meets reminds him of his mother or father and every Italian/American guy or gal he meets reminds him of his siblings. We both had a few glasses at the time, so I don't know if he knew what he was saying, but I believed him anyhow because I felt the same way.

It is also ironic that, at the turn of the century, many Italians left their country to reach the land of opportunity. Indirectly, even though they left their homeland, they ended up presenting their homeland and the family and friends they left behind with the biggest opportunity of their lives. The Italian immigrants in America and all the other immigrants from all the other different European countries helped build America to a phenomenal height by building their roads, their buildings, their banking systems, their sciences, etc., and this country became so rich and powerful that it eventually was able to fund billions of dollars to finance the Marshall Plan after the Second World War. The Marshall Plan would successfully develop the Italian homeland to a point where it was no longer necessary to seek opportunity elsewhere.

This was a great accomplishment that Italian/Americans helped bring about and should be very proud of. No other country on earth ever accomplished such a feat before or since, and my father helped do this for the United States of America *and for his family and friends in Italia.* When the people in this country refer to us, the World War II veterans, as the greatest generation, they should be referring to our fathers and mothers, the early immigrants to this country. These are the people who made this country great and who safeguarded our freedom by giving their sons and daughters to the battle. *God bless them all and keep them by his side.*

THIS NARRATIVE IS COMING TO AN END
(BELIEVE IT OR NOT)

With the passing of Pa, we had to look other places for a comfort zone. Ma loved us dearly and we loved her dearly, but we did not communicate well because of the language barrier. Individually, at least one of us visited Ma every Sunday and hoped she would feed us, but Phyllis and her gang visited *every* Sunday for Sunday dinner, and if the rest of us got there in time, we could enjoy some very good leftovers. With Ma, there would be Allie and Joanna, and Luf who was staying with them, and Phyllis and her family.

Phyllis married an Irishman from Ipswich by the name of John Willey. They married when he came out of the navy, about the same time Bud was getting out of the air force. The wedding was a rather large one with a reception at the Cove Community Center. John and Phyllis had David as their firstborn, and he was certainly a favorite at the Sunday dinners. He and Luf were inseparable, and when Luf didn't have David on his shoulders, Ma had him on her lap constantly. I think Ma loved David the best of anyone. I have to admit he was a cute one. After David, next came their only daughter Patricia, or Patty, as she was commonly called. (Why do most of us only have one daughter?) Then, John Drew, and last was Stephan.

Ma, Allie, and Joanna moved from Dartmouth Street, where we lost Pa, to a newly purchased home on Elliot Street. After a few years there, when Mary and Angelo sold their place in Centerville, Joanna and Allie partnered with them to buy a two-family dwelling at 25 and 27 Lothrop Street, near the beach. Allie, Joanna, and Ma lived on the second floor, where Sunday meals continued with the Willeys and the rest of us who came later for the leftovers. *Just kidding.* Actually, we are a card-playing family, and we would go to visit Ma and get to play a vicious game of pitch, usually with eight players, four partnerships. Mary and Angelo would come upstairs and join us and bring something good to eat, either a dessert or an egg-and-ham frittata. Every Sunday and holiday would be spent this way.

The family was always first, and it seems we all married persons who enjoyed being part of our family. Oh, once in a while, one of the wives was heard to say, "Those Lauranzanos are all alike," but we never took it seriously. Nor did the "sayer" mean anything insulting by it—it just got to be a common saying that we learned to live with. *We heard that it's a rather common saying in Italy, too. I wonder why.*

Lots of time went by the board after Uncle Ralph's passing and Aunt Teresa's passing (Uncle Guido's wife). Over the years, we didn't get to see too much of Uncle Guido anymore, not unless we went to Newport. I think that during the latter years with Pa and Ma in Florida, where Uncle Guido always overstayed his welcome, even his beloved sister could see the end of his visits. Then, Uncle Guido passed away at the age of ninety-nine while dressing one morning in his beloved house that he built so many years ago. Victor and Monica own that house now, while Hector and Polly, his wife, own the bakery and dwelling on Thames Street and snowbird to Florida every winter.

We now were seeing a lot of the Newport kids, Victor and Hector, but not much of Ester and Credo. Hector ran the bakery and Victor was retired, and we still visit back and forth, but age is making it tougher all the time. Victor and Hector served in the navy during the war—being from Newport, where else would they serve. One summer during the war, Uncle Guido got so hard up for help in his bakery that Pa loaned him Bud for the summer to work with his youngest, Credo. They were about the same age. *If nothing else, Credo learned a good game of eight ball.*

In Fall River, Tom sold the bakery and the dwellings and retired. We saw him and Carmella, his wife, on special occasions like wakes, weddings, and once in a while, they showed up for a cookout or two.

Ma passed away rather quietly in the Beverly Hospital in 1971. We were all there when she went to God, but whether she knew we were there I don't know. Luf claims he was talking to her before she passed and maybe she did. I know one thing, though. I know she is talking to God. She raised ten children, helped her husband with his business, cooked his meals, kept his house, and gave him the emotional help everyone needs. Ma pampered her grandchildren and they loved her dearly. She was our mother in every sense of the word, and like all great mothers, they go back to God. We loved her and cherished her and now pray for her eternal rest.

We lost Joe to cancer in 1984, and before he lost his battle, he turned the bakery over to his sons, Peter, Joey, and Jimmie. We all had time to say our goodbyes to Joe, and we did. Joe is now lying with Pa and Ma and has joined them in heaven, I hope.

In 1985, I lost my bride Frances Catherine at the age of sixty-two. We were shocked beyond words because it was so sudden. In fact, it was in the midst of planning Judy's wedding. We had to decide whether to proceed with the wedding or not, but we were sure that she would have wanted us to, so we went on with it.

The reception was at the Hawthorne Hotel in Salem, and it was well run, and a good time was had by all. When my friend Tony Amanti sang "Daddy's Little Girl" and Judy and I danced to it, I could feel that Frances was with us, and Judy and I cried through the whole dance. I have to say it was one of the most emotional times of my life.

Mary and Angelo sold their share of the house on Lothrop Street to Joanna and Allie and moved to Arizona to be close to their children, who had relocated there. Mary died out there and was cremated, and Natalie says her mother will join us after Angelo's death when the both of them come to be buried with us. Angelo is presently living in Maine with Alan and is over a hundred years old at this writing. He'll probably outlive us all. Good luck!

Allie and Joanna sold the house on Lothrop and paid the new owner rent to live downstairs, in Mary and Angelo's old place, to eliminate stairs in their lives. Then, very recently, in the year 2009 at the age of ninety-one, Allie became too tired and left us to occupy her place in heaven. It was not an easy passing—she went through the rigors of old age—but she knew our Lord better then most, and she knew she would eventually be with Him.

Allie was our family. She spoiled us, disciplined us, took care of us, and was happy only when we were. She loved our children just as she loved us. She took care of Pa and Ma in their old age and loved them dearly. Actually, if the truth be known, it should be Allie doing this book, not me, so if this book is not up to her standard or, for that matter, anyone else's, I sincerely apologize. *Allie, you have to know I tried.*

THE EULOGY

When we celebrated Allie's life in church, and as a tribute to her, my nephew Michael, who is currently a judge in the First District Court in Lynn, Mass., authored and delivered this heartfelt eulogy that I repeat here verbatim:

"Good morning, family and friends:

It is fitting that we meet this morning in this wonderful church where our family has both celebrated and mourned for over eight decades. Through the years, we have come to St Mary's to worship, to celebrate first communions, confirmations, weddings, and funerals. Ricky, Dennis, and I were altar boys here. Allie first attended mass in this church over eighty years ago. If you close your eyes, you can imagine young Allie going to church with her sisters Mary and Joanna, perhaps with her brothers Joe, Ned, and Rick, walking up the hill from 36 West Dane Street, turning right onto Cabot Street, until they reached this very place. These brothers and sisters would later include Franny, Luf, Guido, and Phyllis.

Allie was born in 1917, a year before World War I ended. President Woodrow Wilson had just begun his second term. Allie lived through the administrations of sixteen different presidents. She liked some more than she liked others. She usually liked those that had a "D" after their name. In 1917, prohibition was two weeks away. Women would not have the right to vote for three more years.

Allie would have graduated in 1935, some seventy-three years ago. Opportunities for women in the thirties were nothing like they are now. Allie left high school a few months early to work at the soda fountain at the local Woolworth's. She never left the company. Before long, she was promoted to sales clerk, regional buyer in both Boston and New York, and personnel manager at different locations. Finally, she came home and managed the Woolworth's at the North Beverly Plaza.

Can you imagine what Allie would have accomplished if given the opportunities that our generation has had. If Allie had been born a generation or two later, with her intellect and her force of personality and drive, the world would have been her oyster. She was a voracious reader. Crossword puzzles were no match for her. She could discuss any world or national topic in depth. The fact that she also knew the Red Sox starting lineup at any given time only enhanced her in our eyes.

Allie had a great sense of humor. She could be full of mischief. She was a sports fanatic. It was not unusual for Allie to bring a transistor radio to a family event and listen to a Sox game with an earplug. She was an unapologetic Boston sports fan, and like all Boston fans, with apologies to Wayne and Patty Brooks, she hated all New York teams passionately. She passed away on Sunday morning and no doubt was looking down from Heaven and screaming at Bret Farve for throwing that interception that was returned for the touchdown, thereby keeping the Patriots out of the playoffs.

Aunt Allie was all about family. Simply stated, she was the center of our family's universe. Allie had traveled to Italy numerous times over the years and established close relationships with our relatives there. Robin called Sandra, who is the daughter-in-law of Allie's cousin in Italy, to tell them that Allie had passed away. Sandra told Robin that the relatives there refer to Allie as "the soul of our family." Allie's influence is transatlantic.

To her parents, Natale and Colomba, or as we always refer to them as Ma and Pa, she was the dutiful daughter. Most of us in my generation only have fleeting memories of our grandfather, but Allie always spoke so reverently about him. It was so obvious that she was so proud of him for all the sacrifices that he made for his family. Aunt Allie taught us about family and caring so many times, but I personally remember it most when she and Aunts Joanna and Mary took care of Ma when she started to fail. They bought the two-family house on Lothrop Street so someone could watch over her. Those lessons were not lost on those who looked after Aunt Allie these past months; we all owe a great deal of gratitude to Aunt Phyllis, Robin, Judy, Guido, Barbara, Marc, Chris, and Cathy for looking after her.

To Allie's brothers and sisters—Mary, Joanna, Joe, Ned, Rick, Fran, Luf, Guido, Phyllis—she was the glue that held everyone together. Like her parents, Allie was terrified for three of the boys, Ned, Rick, and Luf, who were in the service during World War II. Allie wrote to them two or three times a week so at least one of them would receive a letter from home. She was the family organizer and catalyst, hosting family get-togethers. It was always non-stop. No one could have been a more loyal sister than Allie.

If Allie was the most loving and loyal sister, it comes as no surprise to my cousins that there has never been and never will be an aunt like our Aunt Allie. We were Allie's children. We all have our own Aunt Allie stories of the many kindnesses she showered over us through the years. She attended all of our communions, confirmations, and graduations. She loved all unconditionally, but it never stopped her from telling us what was on her mind. After we started our own families, she was a regular fixture at all children's events. By my count, she had twenty-eight nieces and nephews, forty-five great nieces and nephews. In the last year or so, Enzo, Briggs, and Lucy have joined our family. If they live as long as Allie, they will close out this century. Think about that for a moment.

We cannot speak about Aunt Allie without paying homage to Aunt Joanna. Together Aunts Allie and

Joanna were like the baseball equivalent of Mantle and Maris, a great one-two punch. How many Christmases did we all scurry around the Christmas tree to find out what Aunt Joanna and Allie had given us. We all received our first transistor radios, tape cassette players, and whatever fashionable coat that was available. Any gift from Aunt Allie and Aunt Joanna was precious. I still have the missal they gave me in 1964, some forty-four years ago.

So, we come here today to both grieve and celebrate. Allie had such a wonderful life, full of accomplishment, a life shared with dozens of people that she loved and loved her right back, a life lived by all of us. She would not want us to be sad. She would want us to hold on to one another, to continue to share in each other's joys and support each other when misfortune beckons; after all, that is how she lived her life. This is how she expects us to live ours.

When our final moments of our life come, as surely they will, we will remember all that we hold dear. Our final thoughts will be of those we love: our spouses, our children, our parents, and close friends. For those of us who called Allie sister or aunt, she will be in our final thoughts, and a smile will come to our face.

In a few moments, we will take Allie to her final rest. She has joined Pa and Ma, Aunt Mary, Uncle Joe, Aunt Fran, my mother Alice, Aunt Doris, Paul, and Jill. She is no doubt already taking charge in her usual way. You see, she will always be the center of our family universe. What a life lived.

What a sister.

What an aunt.

What a gift.

God bless you, Aunt Allie."

Thank you, Michael. If I may add my own farewells to your words, *arrivederci* Allie, Pa, Ma, Mary, Joe, Fran, Doris, and Alice, until we meet again.

SOME AFTERTHOUGHTS
(THAT I DID NOT REMEMBER BEFORE BUT
REMEMBER NOW)

During the days of Ned's Jamboree, besides dancing as often as he could, Ned was also a pugilist in training with our neighbor Babe Woods, who was a professional fighter. He lived above Florence Starr's candy store with his father, Henry; his brother "KiKi" (we only knew him by that name); and Henry's girl friend, Leona Ball. Babe had the face of a fighter and was a little punchy, but he knew the fight business and promised to make Ned a champion. Ned sparred a lot and looked very fit, but even so, Babe gave him a training schedule. But Ned told Babe he didn't need his training schedule because he was getting all the training he needed from dancing. Babe asked if he was serious, and when Babe concluded that Ned was serious, he gave Ned the date and place for his first amateur bout, which would take place in Lowell.

Ned showed up for the fight, and Babe and his father, Henry, were in Ned's corner. Ned proceeded to pulverize his opponent for the entire first round; then the round ended and he rested. When the bell sounded for the second round, Ned could not answer the bell, so the referee awarded the fight to his opponent. During the rest period, Ned's legs stiffened, his arms turned to lead, his stomach roiled, and his heart was somewhere else, thus ending a promising pugilistic career and the end of the conception that one could dance his way to a pugilistic championship. The fight game's loss was a gain for the U.S. Army Corp of Engineers.

Uncle Ralph married for the third time sometime after Aunt Giuseppina passed away. He married a widow named Louise. She was somewhat younger than Uncle and liked to move around. As a result, we saw a lot more of him. He and Louise came down to Beverly often and joined us at our cookouts at Mary and Angelo's in Centerville. We liked Louise—she was fun and she treated Uncle well. She particularly got on with the girls since they were in her generation, and they enjoyed her company. Uncle Ralph was his old, robust self and you could hear him well enough when he talked to you, except he never knew your name. When addressing any of us boys, he'd always get it wrong, saying, for example, "... errrr ... you're Americo, sì?" and he'd be talking to Ned. Good old Uncle Ralph, we loved him.

You know, I don't believe I've said enough about The North Shore Bottling Company on Park Street. It was a bigger part of our lives than I have led you to believe. Joe worked there; Jerry Giulebbe, my cousin, worked there; and our close family friend, Fred Valentine, worked there. Off and on, they would pass along some scrub work to me and my friends. I think, for at least four summers running, that was a constant hangout. Joe didn't work there on a steady basis, but mostly only helped Jerry and Fred, who were permanent employees, so to speak. They used to let me inspect the tonic for five cents an hour, out of their own pocket, until they got complaints from customers that the owner, Bob Albert, got wind of, and then it was, "Get lost, Rico."

Then, there was that time in 1943 that Ned and I came home on furlough at the same time, and Joe took us to the Old Howard in Boston to see their strip tease show (for those who don't know what the Old Howard featured). Freddie Valentine was with us. After the show, we went across the street to Joe and Nemo's for their famous hot dogs.

We were sitting in a booth eating heartily, when some guy who was sitting with an out-of-this-world gorgeous woman called me over to him. I went to see what he wanted, and he hauled off and punched me in the jaw. Ned, Joe, and Fred came to my rescue, and other guys joined in the fray to help the guy that cold cocked me, and a real humdinger of a brawl commenced. The police were on their way, so we took off before they came, but not before Ned, the pugilist, had the guy that hit me crying for mercy.

On the way home, I expressed the desire to know why this man hit me, and Ned confessed that he was flirting with the man's out-ofthis-world gorgeous woman. I guess, like they say in the fight game, you have to protect yourself at all times. I had a lump on my jaw for quite a long while after that little fiasco.

The worst time I ever had with Pa, you ask? Well, I was about twelve years old, and I was showing an independent attitude that my Pa did not appreciate. I think he wanted to show me who the boss was, so he assigned me to a task of washing the red stains from the cement on the base of a galvanized fence. This fence is still there, and so is the rust on the cement, but I digress. He gave me a pail of hot water, some lye soap, a scrub brush, and a final instruction of, "Get rid of the stains; they do not look good."

Well, I scrubbed and scrubbed, and my friends Stevie Fortunato and Doobie Carnevale scrubbed and scrubbed, but the stains remained. My friends said maybe we should break off the cement— that would be getting rid of the stains—but I did not think my Pa had that in mind. So, after about four hours of scrubbing, I told my Pa that "I did not think ..." and he replied, "Keep at it." And I countered with, "Like hell I will," and threw the brush away, and ran into the house, up the stairs, and under my bed. Pa chased me and tried dragging me out from under the bed, and Ma, sweet Ma, interceded, and all was forgiven. I thought he was going to kill me. I cried for hours. Ma was there for me yet again. When Allie came home, I was still sobbing, and she asked what happened, and I bellowed out, "ALLIE, PA TRIED TO KILL ME!" I thought I would never forget that day.

Aunt Teresa died comparably young, and I know her family missed her a lot. She was a stabilizing influence in her home. The kids looked up to her and she encouraged them to succeed—not necessarily financially, but with a happy life. She was able to control Uncle Guido. She was easygoing and quiet, but when the gregarious Uncle Guido went too far, she could rein him in. I remember she was an excellent cook. Her specialty was a roast beef roasted in its own juices that melted in your mouth. I can still hear me at her table, "Aunt Teresa, can I have more, please?" That's when I would get a dirty look from Allie and Ma, and Aunt Teresa would say, " No, leave him be, he's a growing boy and needs his nourishment." Good food never escaped my grasp. Never. And Aunt Teresa never refused anyone a second or a third helping.

After Aunt Teresa passed away, sometime later, Uncle Guido found a playmate. She was much younger. He, at this time, was around the octogenarian age and she was in her late fifties or early sixties and currently married to someone else. We never met her—at least, I didn't. But a couple of times, when visiting the boys, Victor and Hector, I used to get a sighting driving down Route 114. He'd be in a car, with his playmate driving the car. I guess she made him happy and fulfilled. He kind of kept to himself during this phase of his life. Other than that, we have some fond memories of him visiting us in Beverly and of us going to Newport.

I don't believe any of us can complain about the life Pa provided for us. We ate well during the great depression, we were clothed and schooled properly, and he showed us that family was the all-important thing in our lives. Pa experienced a great loss in *his* life when he lost his first love. I personally do not believe that he ever got over that loss even though he eventually found Ma. As long as I can remember, I believe I saw something in his eyes that looked longingly for the love that he lost. I remember the look that was always on his face whenever we stopped at Maria's gravesite after twenty years, as though she had left him the day before. I believe he loved Ma in his own way, the way he loved all of us, but I sincerely believe that he loved Maria like no other. Pa, you had the strength to keep that love between you and Maria and the strength to love Ma and the rest of us with no limit.

Thank you, Pa, for all that you have given us. You showed us how to live our lives by example, and although we did not always agree, you were patient and considerate. Thank you for giving us a life that we could pass on to our children. You founded The Lauranzano Clan in Beverly, and may it live forever under your banner.

No. 55 Ma in her favorite pose of all, with a baby. The baby is David Willey, Phyllis` first born and everyone`s favorite at the time. David did have a certain charm and still does.

No.56 Ma at their Florida retreat in Vero Beach dressed in her favorite uniform of the day tending to her plants in the Florida sun. Just like the Italian weather, eh Ma?

*No. 57 This young man is Ma`s second cousin, in Fondi, Italy, who became a
doctor and died at an early age, We believe he was fifty when he died. He was one
of Ma`s favorites. I show him because Ma would have wanted me to.*

*No 58 This is Allie and her favorite uncle, Uncle Ralph, who was visiting Ma and Pa in Florida
and went to Bud and Alice`s wedding with them. Looks like he was having a good time.*

No. 59 Ma is on a ship going to Fondi, Italy in 1961 for the first time since 1912 with a trip sponsored by an Italian organization and she stayed for three months. Ma is the third from the right. Across from Ma is Mrs. Panzera, who lived on Mechanic Street and closest to the camera is Mrs. Sabatini.

This is me in the Beverly High`s new football uniform just before the big game with Salem. I look a little freakish, eh?

No. 61 Aunt Teresa and Angie Carnevale on the right in between is an unknown but I believe she is Angie`s daughter from a previous marriage. They are visiting Ma and Pa at their Florida retreat. Ma and Pa seem to get a lot of visitors in Florida.

No. 62 There`s Pa standing in front of his Florida retreat. He seemed to like spending his winters there, but I think he missed Beverly a lot and his family when he was down there. However, he did have plenty of company down there.

No. 63 Ma and Pa and Uncle Ralph and Aunt Giuseppina on their trip to Canada c1956. I don`t know why they went but it was sponsored by some religious group. Uncle is taking the picture but who is taking the picture of him?

No. 64 A good picture of Uncle Ralph and Aunt Giuseppina standing in a Florida orange grove.

*No. 65 A solo of Pa all dressed and looking like a character actor ready
to step before the cameras. I hope he knows his lines.*

*No. 66 And there`s Uncle Guido at a wedding in Newport looking like he wants
the next dance. Sorry Uncle, I don`t dance. But he did dance quite a bit.*

No. 67 This is Ester and her mama Aunt Teresa (Fiore) Marcucci, husband and daughter to Uncle Guido. They're on the same Canadian trip. They look good together. I do not believe Ester ever got over Aunt Teresa's passing they were very close.

No.68 This is our brother Natale Jr called Ned, he is sitting on our "hang out" stoop on the corner of West Dane and Chase Streets. This was just before he enlisted in the Army in 1938.

*No. 69 Brother in law Angelo Pinciaro looking at the camera and our
brother Luf watching TV at one of Ma`s special Sunday dinners. Enjoying their
coffee probably, just before one of our boisterous family pitch games.*

*No. 70 Allie is in her office at the Woolworth Store in North Bevery their new location. She ran
this store for them even though they sent a manager in. She looks busy and smart, doesn`t she?*

No. 71 Two of Allie's soda fountain girls at Woolworth's on Cabot Street. The girl on the right is Margaret Accomando who became a life long friend of Allie's. The other one is familiar but I can't recall her name.

No. 72 Allie is with another Woolworth lifelong friend, Lorraine Fox posing across the street from the Woolworth store in front of the Gas and Electric Company. Lorraine married an Army major and moved to a station in New Jersey and Allie, my wife Fran and I visited there for a weekend.

No. 73 One of our many outings I keep talking about. This was at Stageport
Park in Gloucester and everyone is present. From left to right, Allie, my wife
Fran, our son Rickey, Velma, looking down reading is Alice, and Angelo.

No. 74 This is another of Ma`s relatives from
Fondi, Italy. She treasured the picture but
never told us who he was.

No. 75 Our brother Giuseppe called Joe holding his son and namesake Joseph Lauranzano, called Joey. They were in their back yard in North Beverly. Sharp dresser was he not? I enjoyed his clothes very much. Didn`t fit me all that well though.

No. 76 There`s a motley looking crew. This is the official Columbus Bakery sponsored ten pin bowling team. Left to right (rear) Luf, Bud and Joe (he bowled with three fingers and a thumb) and in the front is the captain Rico, with the highest average.

No. 77 All the kids visiting Sister Frances. (front) Ned, Allie and Joanna
(middle) Mary, Sister Frances and Rick (rear) Phyllis, Luf, Bud and Joe. This
is all of them. The first generation American Lauranzanos in Beverly

No.78 Pa looking into the camera standing in the front yard. Pa was retired when this was taken and
he just can`t stay away.
Probably there checking on his problem child to see if he was running the bakery properly.

No. 79 These are some of our friends that hung at the corner.
From the left, Louie Gentile, Guy Allaruzzo, Leo DeSantis, and Frank Filtranti.
I probably took the picture c1941

No. 80 Dressed up to kill with no where to go but the corner that was our life at the time, but
we sure did dress up well for Sunday. From left is Rico, Freddie Pasquarelli and Bobby Tate.

No. 81 This is a picture of Fred Pasquarelli that he sent to me in one of his many letters. Good looking guy and a very good friend. We lost Freddie in an accident and we still miss him.

No. 82 Dressed up with no where to go is Rico in 1941. We always dressed up on Sunday. I`m still wearing Joe`s camel hair. He gave it to me after I wore it without him knowing it for my graduation picture.

No. 83 Matt D`Allesandro and I came home on furlough the same time in 1943 and had a great time. Luf is shown with us, he`s still a civilian because he`s waiting to help MacArthur return to the Philippines.

No. 84 Here`s Bobby Tate all dressed up on a Sunday and in the rose garden at our secret paradise that we will not share with the world. It`s God`s little acre created just for us corner rats.

No. 85 In 1941 Frank Filtranti and I are standing under the big willow at our secret paradise.

No 86 In 1941 this is me standing in the rose garden of our secret paradise wearing my football sweater inside out, the sporty way. I earned that sweater the hard way and I wear it proudly.

No. 87 This is my bride that consented to marry me. We married in 1944 in Durham, NC one week before I shipped overseas with the 89ᵗʰ Infantry Division. Together we raised four baby boomers.

No. 88 At Fort Knox in 1943 with a fellow tanker getting ready on a Saturday to go to Louisville for some R and R. aaaahem! Louisville was a great place for R and R

No. 89 Still at Fort Knox with two tankers that were discharged shortly after this picture because of advanced age. They were truck drivers in civilian life and at the time the Army needed drivers.

No. 91 Tank driving was a tough way to make a living 1943, it`s cold and dirty job but someone had to do it. It was much easier in the infantry. Do I look tough or what?

No. 92 Our brother Joe and his wife Laura walk into Joey and Marianne's wedding reception at the Danversport in Danvers.

No. 93 Allie is trying on a jacket she received on Christmas at my house on Woodbury Drive. She enjoyed Christmas and being with family and preparing all the traditional foods like, pasta with shrimp and fried smelt and fried squid (calamare)

No. 94 Ned and Doris and their first born Natale Jr. in my backyard cookout on Woodbury Drive.

No. 95 This is Pa`s birth place in Verzino, Italy visited by Pa`s granddaughter, Robin Lauranzano Gillette and great grand daughters, Regina Lauranzano and Leanne Brooks and his daughter Allie Lauranzano in c2005. Wouldn`t he be pleased.

96 This is a dinner hosted by Vito Squilaci (front left) husband of Carolina Lauranzano of Cortone, Italy. Beverly is well represented with Allie (taking the pic), Robin, Leanne and Regina. The girls are having a good time, but I see Pa sitting with them, don`t you?

No. 97 This is a gracious and wonderful couple, Sandra and Franco Lauranzano of Bari, he is Pa`s great nephew and the grandson of Pa`s brother Giuseppe. Sandra and Franco always host Beverly visitors because they like to and because Sandra speaks fluent English.

No. 98 This was Pa`s residence when he lived there with Maria Leo and when he went there for a prolonged visit. It was renovated by Pa`s great great nephew Gianfranco Iaquinta when he married. This is where Pa built the famous bathroom. Gianfranco is the son of Filomena Lauranzano, sister to Franco.

No. 99 This is an interior view of Pa`s birthplace cave.
Bet it was cool in the summertime

No. 100 A view of Verzino and the realty that is common in the area.

No. 101 Natale Lauranzano, Pa`s nephew, a soldier in the Italian Army stationed in Africa. Father to Michele, Filomena, Carolina and Francesco. A great guy and cuz. We are so glad that we were able to meet him.

No. 102 You see what I mean about Allie? She was there for everyone. Here she is being greeted by our cuz Natale on her visit to Verzino in 2005. We tried to get Natale to visit us but he would not leave his native land and he was kind of up in age and his family would not allow it..

No. 103 This is a picture I would never expect to see. Pa`s great grand daughter sitting with his two great nephews, sons of Pa`s nieces Maria and Francesca, sisters to Natale . Pa never expected his children to ever visit Verzino let alone his great granddaughters. Leanne looks like she belongs there. That`s the Italian in her , I guess.

*No 104 A grand view of Verzino from higher up.
You can see the Chiesa Madre at the top.
And to the left the man himself, born and raised
here, and the founder of our family in Beverly,
MA.
Here`s to you, Dad!*

THE LAURANZANO FAMILY

Book III: Moving On

Moving on in the fifties and sixties was not easy considering that we didn't have Pa to fall back on and we were starting our own families without Pa's guidance and encouragement. Ma was living with Joanna and Allie on Elliot Street. She was still cooking every Sunday meal, or at least she was trying to with Joanna and Allie at her side—very capable cooks in their own right—as advisors of the first class. There were still many family visitors to sample Ma's Sunday meals, followed by the dealing of the cards: pitch, bridge, or gin, but mostly pitch. On Saturday afternoon or evening, one of us would visit Ma and play an Italian card game with her called Scopa, which means sweep. If we had several visiting her at any time, we would play a board game with her, called Pokeno. She loved both games very much.

Luf was still single but wasn't around because, with his masters in English Literature from Columbia University, he was still in New York City, the big apple, teaching high school English. Eventually, however, he found his way home and worked with Joe in the bakery. As you already know, Joe and Joanna, upon Pa's retirement, bought the bakery and dwelling, and a short while later, Joe bought Joanna's share from her and became the sole owner. When Luf came home from New York, he confessed he didn't much like teaching as a career. Joe was in desperate need for experienced help, so he persuaded Luf to work in the bakery as his first baker. Between the two of them, the bakery started to show a lot of life, with assists from Ned and our brother-in-law John Willey.

Joe bought a house in North Beverly on Russell Street with his loving wife, Laura (Mailet), and started raising his family there. His family eventually became the most populated. He and Laura were blessed with:

- Sandra, from Joe's previous marriage, born July 1938
- Peter, born May 1942
- Linda, born June 1948
- Joe, born October 1951
- James, born June 1954

- Laura Jean, born October 1955
- Mary Jane, born November 1958
- Diane, born October 1960

Mary and Angelo Pinciaro had their house in Centerville on Hull Street with a big yard, where we all enjoyed frequent cookouts and get togethers. These cookouts kept our family and friends close through the years. Mary and Ange had three little ones, and they were:

- Paul, born April 1936
- Natalie, born May 1941
- Alan, born September 1956

Natale Jr., or Ned as he was called, and his wife, Doris (Oliver), also had a healthy brood that was raised in North Beverly in a large single home on Raymond Avenue. The children were as follows:

- Aubrey Hawes (from a previous marriage), born June 1941
- Dennis, born February 1947
- Natale III, born February 1955
- Robert, born March 1957
- Nancel, born March 1958

Enrico (that's me) and my wife, Frances Catherine (Grothaus), also had one girl and three boys and Fran's three sisters, and we lived and brought the children up in the Beverly Cove area of Beverly on Woodbury Drive:

- Richard, born in Wilmington, DE, June 1947
- Judith Ann, born January 1954
- Kenneth, born May 1960
- Thomas, born April 1961

And the three sisters:

- Elizabeth, born in Wilmington, DE, in 1936
- Marie, born in Wilmington, DE, in 1939
- Patricia, born in Wilmington, DE, May 1942
- Rafael, or Luf as he is called, remained single and has no offspring.

Guido, or Bud as he is called, and his life mate, Alice (Palmquist), also had one lovely girl and three handsome boys, and they were raised on Butman Street, where the children attended elementary classes at the Hardy School:

- Michael, born January 1954
- Christopher, born December 1954
- Robin, born September 1957
- Marc, born February 1964

Phyllis and her husband, John Willey, lived their married life in the Ryalside part of Beverly in a single stucco-sided house on Marian Street, where they enjoyed raising one girl and three boys:

- David, born August 1956
- John Drew, born March 1958
- Patricia, born November 1959
- Stephan, born May 1965

Even with the raising of my own family in the Cove area of Beverly, I was a guy who was desperate for certain things in the food line, prepared by Ma. One of the dishes I wanted desperately to remain in my life was a peasant dish called Pasta e Fagioli, or as we used to call it when we were growing up, "pastafazool." (I don't know why I mention this at this time—maybe as a change of pace—but for some reason, it seems important to me right now.) For those who do not understand what it is that I am referring to, the exact translation is macaroni and beans. Ma used to make this for us at least two or three times a month when we were growing up, as every Italian mother did for her family throughout the bygone years.

I asked my wife, Frances, to learn how to prepare this dish by asking Joanna, Allie, and/or Ma to show her the intricate secrets that do not show on the recipe. Frances had a few failures at first, but eventually, she did such a good job, I was never without it, and never tired of it, and my family practically grew up on it. Pasta e Fagioli, or macaroni and beans, or pastafazool—call it what you will, it is a dish made from ham bone and a little bit of heaven, and it takes an Italian cook of great skill to prepare it correctly. Pasta e Fagioli, macaroni and beans, or "pastafazool"—it all tastes the same. *Deeeeelicious!*

CHANGES IN BEVERLY
(AFTER THE WAR)

I was in North Beverly one Saturday afternoon, just driving around getting reacquainted with my hometown after being away for six years. I turned up Conant Street and thought I would visit one of my favorite places of all time as a growing child—Hood's Cherry Hill Farm. When I got there, I was struck dumb (some would say that is my natural state)—there was nothing there but empty fields and "for sale" signs. Oh my! What has become of Hood's Cherry Hill Farm?

When we were growing up, this was a favorite place to visit. We used to walk all the way from West Dane Street, down Elliot, up McKay, and down Conant to Cherry Hill. We walked up the long dirt road, through the hay fields, and into the spotless, all-white-interior milking barns, where all the contented cows lived. I think there were at least three of those contented cow barns, and we visited every one of them. Next, we always went to the building where they made ice cream and where we sampled their delicious product (vanilla, of course). After that, we always ran to the hay barn, where we played in the hay and had a barrel of fun. We ended up at the refreshment stand, where there was a free bag of popcorn for each of us. Then, we usually did a funny thing—we watched old people digging in the grassy fields for dandelions. You could make a very good salad with dandelions, and a tasty wine if you could get enough of them.

But now, Hood's Cherry Hill Farm is gone. Hoods moved out, kit and kaboodle. I don't know where they moved this experimental farm to, but I know Beverly should never have let it happen because it made Beverly so much more beautiful. But I suppose that the war had something to do with the closing, as it had for so many other places of interest. I think, though, to this day, Beverly misses Cherry Hill Farm. C'est la guerre!

BUILDING SOMETHING GOOD
(FOR THE COMMUNITY)

I t was in 1951. I was still in art school, and I was living on Chase Street with my wife and children. But on this Saturday, I had just finished my day on the bread truck for Joe, and I was hanging out with Ma and Allie in the kitchen at 36 West Dane, which, as you know, is next to the bakery. And I was eating, as always. Luf was also there with us.

Then, Pepe Carnevale came over to see us. As you also know, he lived across the street with his father, mother, brother Henry, and sister Josephine, and he had just returned from the navy. He asked if Luf and I would come over to his house to attend a meeting. We asked what it was about, and he said they were getting a charter together to form an Italian/American veterans post, and they needed us in order to have the correct amount of signers for the charter, and they also wanted to conduct a meeting to elect officers. We went over to his house for the meeting and found other guys there that we knew very well. There was Peter Fortunato, Tom Mussemeci, Tony and Henry DiRubio, Rudy Millei, John Carnevale, Pat DiPoalo, Rocky Pinciaro, and Joe Fortunato, to name a few, and right there, that night, the Vittori-Rocci Post was born.

We continued to conduct meetings at Pepe's house until we could find a suitable home for the post. We were all continually looking for housing, and finally, Pepe Carnevale came up with Adam Ricci's place on Park Street, on the corner of West Dane, across from the blacksmith. The old, wood-framed building was once part of the Kelleher's Ice and Coal Company, and Adam had bought the property when Kelleher's son John Jr. moved the company out. We rented the upstairs floor, which had a small meeting hall, a small kitchen, and everything else we would need as a starter place. It was still a "dump," but we were desperate.

We had been utilizing this place on Park Street for about a year to hold meetings. During one of our organizational meetings, we decided to name our veteran's post in honor of Beverly's only Congressional Medal of Honor winner, Cpl. Joseph Vittori, and in honor of one who never made it out of Omaha Beach during the invasion of Europe, Pvt. Thomas Rocci. The parents of Corporal Vittori had a home and a farm on Brimbal Avenue and donated a parcel of land to the post so we could build our own facility. This was announced to us at one of our meetings on Park Street, and we all cheered for Mr. and Mrs. Vittori. We decided to build our future home by ourselves on weekends. After all, we were Italian/Americans, so we must have had an abundance of carpenters, masons, plumbers, and workers to erect our building. All we needed was money. Right?

Commander Pepe Carnevale appointed a building committee, which I was on, and we were off to the races. The first thing we did was ask a member, Angelo Clemenzi—a local architect, son, and brother to many brick masons and plasterers—if he would design a building for us in his spare time, and he graciously agreed. We soon had a full set of plans for the building to start construction and a full-blown rendition of the future building that I did from the plans that Angelo supplied. In the meantime, we were running dances and raffles to raise money.

I was at work in Chelsea one day in September of 1953, eating lunch, when me and another guy I worked with started talking about the up-and-coming Marciano-LaStarza fight. The guy I was talking to, Rocco Sposito, told me that the place he brought his cleaning to in East Boston was owned by a person by the name of Mario Zollo. Mario was a personal friend of Marciano and was going to visit Marciano at his Grossinger training camp in a few days. So, one lunch hour, Rocco took me to meet Mario, and when Mario agreed to talk to Rocky about our building fund and his willingness to help, the Rocky Marciano Celebration Day in Beverly was born.

With Mario as the go-between, I was invited by Rocky Marciano to visit him at Grossinger's and talk about a possible visit to Beverly, immediately following the LaStarza fight, to aid our building fund. At this time, I was out of my skin and trying to find a landing spot. I invited Ned and a well-to-do Beverly businessman Nick Ventola to accompany me to help sell our building fund to the heavyweight champion of the world, Rocky Marciano.

We arrived near the training camp on a Thursday, stayed in a motel, visited the camp on Friday and Saturday, made all the necessary arrangements, and had a barrel of fun with Rocky and his entourage. We joked around with visitor Jerry Lewis and had dinner with Ham Fisher, the creator of the comic strip Joe Palooka, who was also visiting. With Rocky's manager Al Weill in concurrence, we agreed that Rocky would be in Beverly following the fight. All we had to do was pick him up in Brockton. Yay!

As everyone knows (even Pa), Rocky beat Roland LaStarza when the referee stopped the fight in the eleventh round and awarded the fight to the champ. Thank God for that.

On the Saturday morning following the fight, we picked "The Champ" up in Brockton, drove him to Beverly, and had a catered lunch at Nick Ventola's home, which was across from Lynch Park. After lunch, we started a motorcade and parade that commenced at Gloucester Crossing and crept down Rantoul Street, with an estimated 35,000 spectators lining both sides of Rantoul Street. The crowd cheered their lungs out for Rocky as he rode by in the back of an open Cadillac convertible with Mayor Wilkinson on one side of him, me on his other side, and Chief of Police Aucone sitting in the front seat with the driver.

The motorcade and parade finally crawled past the reviewing stand that was in front of the Italian Community Center. Rocky left the motorcade and mounted the reviewing stand. The parade continued on and broke up at the train depot on Park Street. Rocky addressed the crowd, and then we hustled him back to Nick Ventola's house. There, we changed our clothes for the dinner at the Salem Armory, where over 1,000 ticket holders were awaiting his arrival. The Salem radio station (WESX) carried the affair live, and the Boston press was there, in droves. Rocky's entire family joined him at the head table—his mother, father, brothers, and wife, Barbara.

The Vittori-Rocci Post got a great deal of publicity from the affair and received almost $10,000 for the building fund. And I had the time of my life getting to know the greatest fighter of all time, the undefeated heavyweight champion of the world, Rocky Marciano. How great is that? *It's like Pa getting to meet Primo Carnera before the Max Baer fight, back in 1935.*

I NOTICED CHANGES
(ON RANTOUL STREET)

One of the more noticeable changes on Rantoul, and one that I was sorry to see, was the disappearance of Kramer's Department store on the corner of West Dane, across from Ricci's Market. Kramer occupied what I always thought was the prettiest and the best built building on Rantoul Street in the Italian/American neighborhood (with maybe the exception of Kransburg Furniture Store). It was clean, the building was well constructed, and Kramer competed with the uptown stores. There was nothing else like it in the neighborhood. The war must have caused it to go out of business, and the neighborhood lost a good friend. I will always remember Kramer's and Jean Cappi, who worked there for years and was a personal friend to my older sisters and to our entire family.

To make matters even worse, the building was bought by the Sciarcca family, which opened a market there, where they specialized in the sale of rotten fruit and produce and old meat. I know this to be true because my mother told me it was true. Ma continued to buy her meat from Jake and Albert Ricci from across the street. Of course, the Ricci boys sold a lot of our bread, so they had to be good, right? Anyway, we knew that the Sciarcca store would not be long for this world, and it wasn't. It closed its doors, and the building was bought by Fred Paglia, who owned and operated the Venician Café near the Gloria Chain Store, down a way on Rantoul Street. Mr. Paglia remodeled the building, and he somehow got the smell out and opened a Ristorante Italiano that started a new era in our neighborhood. It was called ... **Freddie's**. The Lauranzano clan almost regarded **Freddie's** as their own.

Joe was a regular customer and could be found there whenever he wasn't working. When Joe retired, Freddy Paglia had already passed on and his son-in-law Colo DiStefano was the proprietor, along with Freddie's daughter Minnie. Colo DiStefano and Joe were very good friends, and Joe was at *Freddie's* so often that we used to kid him about having a financial interest in the place. It wasn't long, however, before we all started to meet there practically every Saturday afternoon for pizza or tripe and beer. We'd watch games there, meet all the neighbors who were in and out of the place, and argue about anything that would come up. It became the meeting place for the Lauranzanos and the neighborhood, so to speak. Though I was sad at seeing Kramer's leave our neighborhood, and hated the sight and smell of Sciarcca's, I was most happy with the introduction of **Freddie's Italiano Ristorante** to our neighborhood, where we had some great family get-togethers and a lot of fun. Thank you, Freddy, wherever you are.

... AND ON CABOT STREET

About this time, not long after the war, I walked uptown along Cabot Street, as we always did before the war when we were younger. But like other places and things that were changed by the war, it was not the same. The Ware Theater, which was so important to us during our youth, changed its name to Cabot Cinema and was showing only "arty" pictures or old classics. Further down, Almy's Department Store moved out of its old place, and when the National Bank burned down, they changed its face with their new facility. Frank Woolworth and my sister Allie moved their store to a shopping center in North Beverly, with a Zayer's Discount Store and a Star's Super Market as their new neighbors—that was the start of putting the small stores on Rantoul Street out of business.

Back on Cabot Street, we found that WT Grant had closed their store, and Davidson's Department Store also closed. The Larcom Theater closed its glorious doors, and of all places, with so many fond memories, "The Greeks" closed their ice cream parlor. *Ye, Gods, where will the kids bring their dates?* On Ellis Square, Goodwin's sold out and was called something else, and it wasn't even a bus stop anymore. How many people remember Rope's Drug Store on the corner of Broadway and Cabot Streets, occupying the same building that's there now? It's an old building and a familiar sight in Old Beverly, across the street from the City Hall.

On my many walks "uptown," it became obvious to me that all the casualties did not occur on the battlefields of Europe or the Pacific. We have but to look at Main Street USA to see the many more casualties that fell by the wayside that we will painfully miss till the day we die.

CABOT STREET
IT __WAS__ BEVERLY!

Cabot Street before the war was the center of Beverly, especially on Saturday night. It was the *real* Beverly. I think every family living in Beverly went uptown to shop on Saturday, day or night. Sooner or later, if you stayed on the corner of Federal and Cabot in front of Woolworth, you would eventually get to see everyone in Beverly, which we did on many an occasion. And on those many occasions, I think we actually did see everyone in Beverly. The Woolworth on Saturday night was always packed with people, and Allie's soda fountain was standing room only. And when you walked by WT Grant's store, you would invariably smell the peanuts roasting. Oh, what an aroma that was. Never to be forgotten. What is more compelling then an aroma of roasting peanuts, or warm bread?

In those early days, not having a car to drive your date around, you walked uptown with your date, sat in The Greeks after a movie or a church dance, and treated your date to whatever she wanted. You would walk her home and get a lip kiss goodnight. How good was that? You wouldn't know it to see Cabot Street after the war, but the sidewalks of uptown Cabot Street before the war were like Times Square in New York City—crowded with people, wall to wall, overflowing onto the street, all carrying shopping bags, big smiles, and a bigger "hello."

Christmas Season was something else to see and experience on Cabot Street— the snow, the lights, the decorated windows, the Salvation Army volunteers, and the carolers all contributing to a very homey Beverly Christmas. I have never again, after the war, experienced the color and realism of Christmas as a part of old Beverly's on Cabot Street. The warmth I felt in Almy's, for instance, when purchasing a gift for Ma, and then walking out with my package onto Cabot Street, and walking home through the snow, and meeting all the people going to and fro. With an occasional horse and sleigh going by, carrying a slew of people snuggled in the hay shouting

"Merry Christmas" to everyone, you would really feel Christmas to your very bones. When I walked down West Dane from Cabot, I would see all the houses with their Christmas trees lit up and showing through their front windows, and I would feel a little lonesome. And then, I would walk into our yard and through the kitchen door into Ma's warm kitchen, and I knew I had a home, too, and I knew Christmas in Beverly was for real.

God bless the Beverly I once knew, and I wish everyone today could experience what we had in old "uptown" Beverly. I don't know—underneath everything, maybe it's still there.

CHANGES IN PA'S BAKERY
PA WOULD UNDERSTAND

The stores on Rantoul Street were closing their doors because of deaths, taxes, and supermarkets opening up in Beverly. There was The Star Market in North Beverly; The A & P on Gloucester Crossing; Henry's Market, also in North Beverly; Demoulas Market in Danvers; and others. Because they had so much volume, these stores could cut prices so much that our stores on Rantoul Street could not compete—even Charlie Bucci had to close up his store. And as a result of all these stores closing, Columbus Bakery suffered. What saved the bakery was a man named Sam Lena, who started a chain of Sub Shops and agreed that Joe would supply all the bread for his shops. This was a long, French-style loaf, which was cut four ways by the sandwich maker and became very popular.

Joe worked long and hard to perfect this product and ended up discarding Pa's brick oven and replacing it with a circular-type oven, with steam, to maintain a consistency. Business started booming again, and there were new mixers, etc.—in fact, he made his bread without a human hand touching the product, and the name was changed to The Columbus Baking Company. They delivered the bread to the sub shops early in the morning—5:00 AM—and they were finished by 10:00 AM. It just was not the same, and I could never accept the new concept. But time does go forward, and you have to accept the changes that the war brought forth.

Sam Lena was a lifesaver—or I should say a bakery saver—and he and Joe got on famously. You have to hand it to Joe—he wasn't always Mr. Nice Guy, but he knew only one way to run the bakery, and that was the hard way. Times do change, and Joe had to change with it, and I don't think anyone else could have saved the bakery after the war but Joe. And that's all I'm going to say about the bakery. It's like I used to tell Pa in the *ooooold* days, "Pa, there are other things in life besides the bakery." He never did believe me.

OTHER CHANGES ...

There were other changes on Rantoul Street, like the closing of the Rantoul Hardware that was founded by the Manual brothers, David and Otis. They passed on, and that was a big loss for Beverly. The Black and White Swing Band that they founded back in the 1930s is still going strong, and that is a good thing. It is being carried on by their nephew Al Mitchell and most of the original players. They go way back to 1936, when Pa hired them to play at Mary's wedding. They were a young band then and are still going strong—shows how good they are.

The Blackstone Café, located in the Cosby Block, is no more. That is a place I remember because it's the first place that *I* know of that had a sign "Booths For Ladies," with a hand pointing to the rear of the building. When I was about ten or twelve, I sold the evening edition of the *Boston Daily Record* on the streets of Beverly, and the Blackstone was one of my favorite places to sell my papers.

Ah, the Boston Record's evening edition, with half the Red Sox box score on the back page because the game was still in progress when the paper went to press. Leo Eagan and Austin Lake's sports columns—oh, how they got on Ted Williams' case. They were the main reasons why Ted hated the Boston press. But it sold papers, and I did okay with that. I sold about fifty to seventy-five a night. It kept me in movie money, and they knew me in all the barrooms, especially the Blackstone. The paper cost five cents, and tips were good, depression or not. The Blackstone Café, along with the Boston Record, was the end of an era for me.

Along with super chain stores driving the independent storeowner out of business, so did the drugstore chains drive the independent drugstores into oblivion. One of the victims was our favorite family drugstore, Nick Galluzzi's Rantoul Pharmacy. Nick was part of us growing up. He never refused to fill a prescription, whether you had the money or not. Whenever the doctor left our house and left a prescription to be filled, Ma would give one of us the money and the prescription and off we would go to Nick's. If he was closed, we would call him, and he would come down to the store to fill it. What a guy! Now, the store is gone, and so is Nick Galluzzi, our neighborhood druggist.

MOVING ON

Although we will miss all these former friends and neighbors for one reason or another, we do have to move on to the next generation and wish for something better for them. I don't know what future we will make for our children, but I do hope that it will be something they can look back on with fond memories, as we have done with our past.

I don't know if we were so distracted by the war we had to endure that our children missed something from us that we should have been able to give them. I hope this is not the case, and that we were able to give them a better life, and that they, in turn, will be equipped to serve their children in an even better way.

In any case we do have to suck it all up and move on. And I say amen to that! – Enrico G. Lauranzano

The Beginning

ACKNOWLEDGEMENTS

Because one cannot write a book alone I do have to take this time to thank some people for giving me the help I needed in the writing of this story about The Lauranzano Family. For instance I had help from some Lauranzanos in Italy, like our cousin Natale in Verzino who passed on a lot of information about the early Lauranzanos. in Longobucco, as well as Verzino. Natale even did some traveling to get information for this book. Unfortunately, Natale passed away and will not see the finish of the project.

I want to thank Natale's son Francesco (called Franco) who lives in Bari, Italy who contributed information and family trees that were more than just helpful.

I want to thank Verzino's Mayor, Italo Russo and his librarian who agreed to honor Pa in their library with the picture I drew and colored of their church, Chiesa Madre, that remembers Pa to the people of Verzino.

Here in this country I want to thank my daughter Judy Lauranzano Rich and my niece Robin Lauranzano Gillette for helping me with the images that you see in this book.

My editor Sandra Goldin Zaccaghrini became so familiar with our family she thinks of herself as a family member. Thank you Sandy you were great, with out you this project would have been much more difficult to complete.

Roger Langley, my computer whiz kid, who kept me in constant touch with my computer. Thank you, Roger.

I want to especially thank my nephew Michael Lauranzano who encouraged and urged me to start this project before the memories were lost and who wrote and delivered the eulogy you see verbatim in the book.

Last, but not at all least, I want to thank my wife Donna who encouraged me throughout and because I wanted to many times, would not allow me to quit.

Thank you all for all the help and encouragement you gave me. I can now go back to my true love of drawing and coloring and start another project before I get too old.

Enrico G Lauranzano

No 105 This is a group image of The Lauranzano Family. Well some of them, anyhow.
This was taken at a summer reunion in 2004 at the Cove Community Center.

ABOUT THE AUTHOR

Enrico G Lauranzano was born in Beverly, MA eighty six years ago where he received his primary education. He attended and graduated from a four year art course at Vesper George School Of Art in Boston, MA and previous to that attended a two year course at the Philadelphia School of Fine Arts.

This is Mr Lauranzano's first attempt at writing. He took up this challenge when he was convinced that memories had to be put in writing before they all became lost to us. "The Lauranzano Family Story" became his project with much help from many people. Sub-titled "From The Mountains Of Calabria" it becomes primarily his father's story.

Mr Lauranzano's main interest is in the art of drawing and coloring and is consuming his life when he is not writing this narrative. His artwork can be seen on his website where you can also communicate with him.   www.artbyeglauranzano.com

SYNOPSIS

In **The Lauranzano Family Story**, Mr. Lauranzano pays tribute to his family in the greatest way possible, he keeps alive the memory of those who have gone before him and gives the gift of these memories to those who came behind. Starting with his grandfather in Italy and the birth of his father there, he takes his father as the keystone, bringing to life this amazing man's experiences with a storyteller's flair and weaving them and those of his family into the American experience. This is not just the story of one immigrant family. Many others will be touched by their own family memories and by their pride in this country while reading this wonderful saga. And the Lauranzano family forever will have a record of the great love and the great talent that grew them.